A Living Faith

A Living Faith

A DEVOTIONAL JOURNEY THROUGH JAMES

Stanley D. Gale

Reformation Heritage Books
Grand Rapids, Michigan

A Living Faith
Copyright ©2023 by Stanley D. Gale

Reformation Heritage Books
3070 29th St. SE
Grand Rapids, MI 49512
616–977–0889
orders@heritagebooks.org
www.heritagebooks.org

Printed in the United States of America
23 24 25 26 27 28/10 9 8 7 6 5 4 3 2 1

Library of Congress Cataloging-in-Publication Data

Names: Gale, Stanley D., 1953- author.
Title: A living faith : a devotional journey through James / Stanley D. Gale.
Description: Grand Rapids, Michigan : Reformation Heritage Books, [2023]
Identifiers: LCCN 2023030320 (print) | LCCN 2023030321 (ebook) | ISBN 9798886860726 (paperback) | ISBN 9798886860733 (epub)
Subjects: LCSH: Bible. James—Devotional literature.
Classification: LCC BS2785.54 .G35 2023 (print) | LCC BS2785.54 (ebook) | DDC 227/.9106—dc23/eng/20230814
LC record available at https://lccn.loc.gov/2023030320
LC ebook record available at https://lccn.loc.gov/2023030321

For additional Reformed literature, request a free book list from Reformation Heritage Books at the above regular or email address.

For Cheryl,
who encouraged me to write a book on James,

and for Linda,
who suggested a devotional format

Contents

Acknowledgments

I want to acknowledge three strands braided together that brought about the publication of this book. The first is the personal encouragement from others who appreciated my teaching on James, particularly my wife, Linda and our longtime friend Cheryl Schultz. A writing project rising from my own initiative is one thing, but to be asked to write something by those who think I have something to contribute is quite another. The second strand is Reformation Heritage Books. To be honest, I never expected them to pick up the project and was shocked by how quickly they jumped on board. I am delighted to be working again with Jay Collier and Annette Gysen. The third is Meadowcroft Presbyterian Church. I filled in for the pastor while he went on a three-month sabbatical. That gave me the opportunity to preach through James and engage in further study of both content and continuity. The enthusiasm of the congregation humbled me but also served as an impetus to write the book you hold.

Introduction: Living Faith

The epistle of James reminds us that all theology is practical theology. God's written Word makes demands of us for what we believe and how we behave. His truth is not abstract but is to be applied, not to puff up but to build up.

James calls us to a life of faith. Faith is both passive and active. On the one hand, it is passive in the sense that it is received as a gift of God, a display of the Spirit's regenerating work in our lives. While we were dead in sin, God came to us and made us alive in Christ. With that grace of faith, we embrace Jesus Christ for salvation.

On the other hand, faith is active in that it expresses itself in a new relationship with God. We exercise faith, bringing it to bear and working out our salvation. Salvation is not by our works or even by our works prompted by faith. But authentic faith, faith given by God, will be authenticated by its deeds. As James puts it, "Faith by itself, if it does not have works, is dead" (James 2:17). And if it is dead, then it has no power to save: "What does it profit, my brethren, if someone says he has faith but does not have works? Can faith save him?" (v. 14).

James conveys great pastoral concern in his letter. He writes to believers in order to minister to them in their suffering. But his intention is more than extending comfort. He is concerned that we capitalize on the trials we face in pursuit of the purposes of God for us in them. He leads us in how to do that.

Prominent throughout the epistle is faith. The pressure of trials both proves and improves faith. It proves faith in that it demonstrates the tenacious grace of God. Genuine faith will endure under trial (see Luke 8:13–15). Trials improve faith in that they provide weight resistance by which faith is strengthened to rest and rely ever increasingly on Christ, the object of our faith. In pastoral fashion, James's letter is filled with instruction, care, warnings, illustrations, and examples of living for Christ's kingdom amid the kingdom of this fallen world.

This devotional will take us through the entire epistle of James. It won't be exhaustive, delving into every detail, but it will be exhilarating as our Father in heaven leads us and counsels us in the trenches of life common to all. Each devotion will be followed by two questions aimed at doing the word (see James 1:22), whereby we look to put into practice what we have heard.

Hearing God's word and putting it into practice is an individual responsibility. We cannot exercise another's faith. But we are part of a community of faith and are to stimulate one another to love, what James calls "the royal law" (James 2:8), and good deeds. This devotional can be used privately, but its brevity is well suited for meeting with fellow believers to read the segment aloud, discuss together, and support each other in prayer and encouragement.

I urge you to read the epistle of James in one sitting, as you would read a letter written to you by a dear friend. Get the lay of the land through the bigger picture in preparation for our dive into the details, with an eye to navigating life in this fallen world animated by faith and guided by wisdom in our Lord Jesus Christ.

Take on Trials

... when you fall into various trials ...

—JAMES 1:2

Several years ago, a Christian writer penned an article entitled "Don't Waste Your Cancer." The upshot was that the trial that cancer brings is not simply to be weathered, endured with a stiff upper lip. It is to be welcomed, received with a sense of anticipation.

James takes it a step further when he says, "My brethren, count it all joy when you fall into various trials" (James 1:2). Not only are we to welcome trials, we are to welcome them with open arms, not resigning ourselves to them but actually rejoicing in them.

Consider what adversities you are dealing with right now. Perhaps it's a diagnosis of cancer, or sudden financial disaster, or heart-wrenching divorce. Would you characterize your reaction as joy? Likely not, yet that is exactly where faith leads you, and not as some sort of happy-face, head-in-the-sand religious zealot. Rather, faith leads us to a joy that belies the tragedies that befall us, a joy expressed in part by the Old Testament prophet Habakkuk:

> Though the fig tree may not blossom,
> Nor fruit be on the vines;
> Though the labor of the olive may fail,
> And the fields yield no food;
> Though the flock may be cut off from the fold,
> And there be no herd in the stalls—
> Yet I will rejoice in the LORD,
> I will joy in the God of my salvation.
>
> The LORD God is my strength;
> He will make my feet like deer's feet,

> And He will make me walk on my high hills.
> (Hab. 3:17–19)

To put it in contemporary terms, "Though my bank account is empty, my cupboard bare, and my prospects dim, yet I will find joy in the Lord my God. He is my delight, my sufficiency, my strength; and in Him I will persevere."

This sentiment reflects a common theme of the Bible for those whose God is the living Lord. James brings it to the fore as the first word for believers who are uprooted and oppressed. He fits us with the spectacles of faith. These lenses are not rose colored. Quite the contrary—they give us greater visual acuity for understanding the days and navigating the paths of life in this fallen world. Through faith, we see suffering in all its harshness. The lens of faith enables us to see even the direst affliction as the soil from which the blossom of joy emerges with the fragrance of grace.

Finding joy in trials does not happen automatically. Likely, our default response to ordeal is fear or worry or dread, a reflex that balks at the trial, like touch to a flame. That's why James will explain to us how to capitalize on our hardships, contrary to our impulse.

But for now, he simply says, "Count it all joy" when we encounter the unwanted guests of trials along the way. He wants us to don those glasses of faith that will enable us to perceive benefit in it and to persevere through it with joy and great expectation.

DOING THE WORD

1. How does faith transform trials?
2. What is your greatest obstacle to finding joy in trials?

Every Joy or Trial

Count it all joy.

—JAMES 1:2

"Trials" carries a negative connotation, however the word is used. Legal trials are anxiety producing and menacing. Time trials stretch us to the extreme and place us in opposition to other athletes. Trials of life weigh us down, rob us of peace, and threaten our security. By their nature, trials provoke unpleasantness and hardship. Peter describes the response to trials as being "grieved" by them (1 Peter 1:6). Trials bring with them the danger of growing weary and losing heart.

Yet James looks us in the eye and with a straight face tells us to "count it all joy" (James 1:2) when we encounter trials of various kinds. He is not just talking about nuisance difficulties, like a fender bender or getting locked out of the house, where we are more likely to be able to grin and bear it. No, James has in mind the gamut of trials that we meet in the course of life. Such hardship comes in all shapes and sizes, intensities and durations. In his letter James gives us a sampler of trials when he writes of persecution, sickness, financial struggle, and temptations.

How can we possibly find joy in suffering? We begin to answer that question when we recognize the hand from which the trial comes to us. Later in his epistle, James will hold up Job as an example of someone who persevered through affliction. But James wants us not so much to look at Job as he wants to direct our attention to where Job is looking: "You have heard of the perseverance of Job and seen the end intended by the Lord—that the Lord is very compassionate and merciful" (James 5:11). Job's focus is on the God he knows to be compassionate and merciful and who is at work according to His perfect purpose.

If we would not only endure trial but somehow find a peculiar joy in it, we must see through faith the hand of God our Father Almighty that extends it to us. When Job had been beset by one affliction after another, surely what James would describe as trials of various kinds, Job's wife urged him to "curse God and die!" (Job 2:9). How did Job respond? He said, "You speak as one of the foolish women speaks. Shall we indeed accept good from God, and shall we not accept adversity?" (v. 10). Job couches his comment in terms of foolishness as opposed to wisdom. Foolishness speaks its own mind. Wisdom speaks in the fear of the Lord, something that James will have much to tell us about in his letter.

James, as well as Job, understood that God is sovereign over all that comes to pass, and everything serves His good and perfect will. Frances Ridley Havergal, nineteenth-century composer of classic hymns such as "Take My Life and Let It Be," grasped this foundational truth. In her hymn "Like a River Glorious" she wrote, "Every joy or trial falleth from above, traced upon our dial by the Sun of Love."

We see this principle most vividly represented in our Lord Jesus, "who for the joy that was set before Him endured the cross, despising the shame" (Heb. 12:2). Jesus's food was to do the will of Him who sent Him. Like with our Lord, the joy is not in suffering but in the purpose of the God we know and love.

DOING THE WORD

1. Describe a time when you were tempted to grow weary and lose heart in trials.
2. How does looking at God cast trials in a different light?

Exercising Faith

... the testing of your faith ...

—JAMES 1:3

What makes muscles grow stronger? One way is simply through use. You won't find "couch potato" on a list of workout routines. A way to build muscle is through weight resistance, but that resistance must be appropriate. If you curl a dumbbell that is too light, you won't realize much benefit. But if the weight is just beyond your reach so that it requires effort, your muscles will develop and strengthen.

Trials offer weight resistance to our faith in order to strengthen it. And the weight they offer has been measured for us by our God. He knows the degree of our spiritual development and brings trials tailored to us to mature us in the faith.

James describes this weight resistance as *testing*. He speaks of both the exercise and the outcome when he says that "the testing of your faith produces patience. But let patience have its perfect work, that you may be perfect and complete, lacking nothing" (James 1:3–4). The testing of our faith through the weight resistance of trials strengthens it and leads to Christian maturity. Twice James uses the word "perfect." The term he uses carries the sense of a goal reached. He reinforces the idea by speaking positively of "complete" and negatively, "lacking in nothing."

What James is saying is that the trial you are facing right now is tailored to your level of spiritual maturity for the purpose of growing you in Christlikeness. The Holy Spirit is your trainer. Your job is to show up, embracing the trial as given by God, exercising the faith He has worked in you, and cooperating with the Spirit.

God's Word reminds us that it is the Spirit who forms Christ in us, but that does not make us passive for our spiritual development. When

Paul writes, "I can do all things through Christ who strengthens me" (Phil. 4:13), he encourages us in the ability to do what God calls us to do, and he also engages us as the doer ("I can do"). Paul describes his own labors as "striving according to His working which works in me mightily" (Col. 1:29). We are the ones who exercise faith.

How do we exercise faith? James gives us our starting point, where to begin when we encounter trials. He has told us to "*count* it all joy" (James 1:2; emphasis added). He uses a word that takes us to the exercise mat of the mind, where we prepare ourselves to deal with the heft the trial brings to us. To "count" is to regard, to adopt the position, to bring a perspective to bear for the trial at hand. James goes on to say, "Knowing that the testing of your faith produces..." (v. 3). Again, he appeals to the mind for the work to be done.

What exactly do we know? What faith perspective are we to put in place to govern our opinion about the trial and to handle it for spiritual growth? We've already noted two stretching exercises for the strengthening of faith. One, we recognize that the trial at hand has come from the hand of our sovereign God and Father. Two, we operate in faith believing that His purposes for our growth in the grace and knowledge of the Lord Jesus Christ are at work, tailored to our needs.

DOING THE WORD

1. What is God's ultimate purpose in the trials you face?
2. What attitude adjustment do you need to make to benefit from trials?

Chapter 4

A Word to the Unwise

If any of you lacks wisdom …

—JAMES 1:5

A family had an emergency at their home. Their furnace had quit on them. Outside temperatures were in the teens. Inside, their thermostat read forty-one degrees. They called for repair, and a service tech showed up. He took a look at the furnace, pulled off a faceplate, and pushed a button. The furnace roared to life. The service tech then presented the bill—$245. The homeowner railed, "You've got to be kidding. You weren't even here for five minutes. All you did was push a button. I could have done that." The tech said, "True, but you needed to know what button to push and when to push it."

The service tech displayed not just knowledge; he displayed know-how. James calls that "wisdom," and he will develop the concept throughout his letter. Wisdom is necessary to handle trials so that we benefit from them for our spiritual growth.

James already told us that when facing trials, we need to employ the perspective God gives us. Now James goes on to address how we put that knowledge to use. "If any of you lacks wisdom, let him ask of God, who gives to all liberally and without reproach, and it will be given to him" (James 1:5). To handle the trial adroitly, we need wisdom. Wisdom looks to God, learns from God, and leans on God.

I am what you might call directionally challenged. For me the greatest technological advance is GPS. The thing is, the Bible says we are all directionally challenged. As the proverb puts it, "There is a way that seems right to a man, but its end is the way of death" (Prov. 14:12). We all have a built-in misalignment. Left on our own, we can easily go astray. That is precisely why we need wisdom.

Wisdom is skill in living biblically. That skill is no more urgently needed than in the turmoil of trials. When we panic, we can act reflexively and impulsively. But that sort of reaction does not usually lead us in the way our God wants of us and certainly not in a way to capitalize on the trial He has brought to us and that carries His purposes for us in it.

For wisdom to function as it should, it must be calibrated properly. A compass functions properly when it is oriented to due north. Due north for wisdom is the fear of the Lord. "The fear of the LORD is the beginning of wisdom, and the knowledge of the Holy One is understanding" (Prov. 9:10), the proverb informs us.

The idea behind this fear is that God be given the glory that is His due. It is to acknowledge Him for who He is, in all He reveals Himself to be. With a proper view of God comes a proper view of self. God is the creator; we are the creature. Operating in the fear of the Lord brings that distinction, dependence, and devotion to bear in navigating the trials of our lives.

Where do we get wisdom? We find it where faith points us, to our God and Father.

> Yes, if you cry out for discernment,
> And lift up your voice for understanding,
> If you seek her as silver,
> And search for her as for hidden treasures;
> Then you will understand the fear of the LORD,
> And find the knowledge of God.
> For the LORD gives wisdom;
> From His mouth come knowledge and understanding.
> (Prov. 2:3–6)

We are not alone in handling trials.

DOING THE WORD

1. Why is wisdom necessary for handling trials?
2. How does wisdom relate to the fear of the Lord?

Chapter 5

Wisdom's Well

Let him ask of God.

—JAMES 1:5

We need wisdom to navigate the trials of our lives. James makes it clear that wisdom comes from God. We gain that wisdom from God by *asking* Him for it. "If any of you lacks wisdom, let him ask of God, who gives to all liberally and without reproach, and it will be given to him" (James 1:5). James expresses this asking as a command to be obeyed and something we need to persist in. He describes what we might call importunate prayer, a relentless pursuit of God, what Isaiah characterizes as giving God no rest (Isa. 62:6–7).

Really what God wants is our attention—our rapt attention. He wants us to see Him through the eyes of faith: His presence with us, His grace sufficient for us, His word that lights our path, His hope that is an anchor to our soul. He wants us to draw near to Him, taking courage in His promises and finding joy in His purposes for us in Christ through the trial. He wants us to hear Him when He says,

> Fear not, for I am with you;
> Be not dismayed, for I am your God.
> I will strengthen you,
> Yes, I will help you,
> I will uphold you with My righteous right hand.
> (Isa. 41:10)

He wants us to heed the words of His Son: "Peace I leave with you, My peace I give to you; not as the world gives do I give to you. Let not your heart be troubled, neither let it be afraid" (John 14:27).

Wisdom positions us with our God. In our weakness, we will know His might. In our fear, we will know His peace. In our foolishness, we will know His discernment doled out as needed, manna for the day at hand.

James assures us that we will not find the well dry when we approach it for wisdom. I mentioned that I am directionally challenged. A fellow pastor and I would head out to lunch at a place we both enjoyed near where he lived. Invariably, I would need to ask for turn-by-turn directions, even after having gone there several times. My friend would patiently tell me which way to go. It would be a bit embarrassing for me to ask for directions *yet again*, but my friend always responded with as much information as I needed and without recrimination. That's how James describes our interactions with our heavenly Father. God will respond to our request for wisdom generously and without reproach.

Our Father never says, "Are you back again?" or "How dumb can you be?" He tends to His children in their foolishness and according to their need. He knows our frame. He is responsive to our plea.

When we ask for wisdom, what might we say? There is no formula, no script. It's simply a matter of being real before our God. No Christian happy face. No stiff upper lip. We simply lay the trial out before Him, being honest about our struggles, our doubts, our fears. If we need a tutorial in this sort of conversation with God, we need look no further than the Psalms. The book of Psalms gives us the vocabulary for praise, confession, lament, confusion, doubt, thanksgiving, and petition as we wrestle with God in the direction of hope.

DOING THE WORD

1. Why does God want us to ask for wisdom?
2. How does God want us to ask for wisdom?

Chapter 6

Believing Prayer

Let him ask in faith.

—JAMES 1:6

We knew there had to be a catch. James has guaranteed that God will dispense the wisdom we need to handle the trials we encounter "liberally and without reproach" (James 1:5). There will be no rationing from the well of wisdom. It's ours for the asking. But now he shows us the fine print: "But let him ask in faith, with no doubting, for he who doubts is like a wave of the sea driven and tossed by the wind. For let not that man suppose that he will receive anything from the Lord; he is a double-minded man, unstable in all his ways" (vv. 6–8).

What are we to make of this proviso? I don't know about you, but it makes me nervous. I have plenty of doubts at times. In fact, trials can bring an infestation of doubt. What exactly is James saying? Actually, nothing that should surprise us.

We have noted that the book of James is not primarily about trials, although trials and adversity feature prominently. Nor is James primarily about wisdom, although wisdom is an oft-mentioned topic. Rather, his pastoral letter is primarily about faith, what genuine faith looks like and how it operates in everyday life. So it's no surprise that when James speaks of prayer, he incorporates faith. At the close of his letter, James will present a tutorial on prayer. There he refers specifically to "the prayer of faith" (James 5:15).

Prayer does not work as an incantation, where we utter the right words or mindlessly repeat empty phrases. Here, James echoes the teaching of Jesus in the Sermon on the Mount:

> And when you pray, do not use vain repetitions as the

> heathen do. For they think that they will be heard for their many words.
>
> Therefore do not be like them. For your Father knows the things you have need of before you ask Him.
>
> (Matt. 6:7–8)

Real prayer is infused with faith. Such faith knows that God exists, believes that He hears, and trusts that He will answer in keeping with His perfect purposes. In fact, God has established prayer as His means to His ends.[1] He actually ordains our feeble, ignorant utterances for the accomplishment of His outcomes. James will make this vivid through his explanation of believing prayer and the example of Elijah later in his letter. Prayer is the voice of faith.

When James stresses asking in faith "with no doubting" (James 1:6), he is not teaching what we sometimes hear: "If only you had enough faith, your child would be healed," or "If only you had more faith, your bank account would be full." James's point is not the amount of our faith but the object of our faith. He urges a faith that fully and exclusively rests in the true and living God. We are not to be double-minded. We are not, as Elijah pressed when challenging the prophets of Baal, to "falter between two opinions" (1 Kings 18:21) or, as Jesus put it, to "serve two masters" (Matt. 6:24).

James's illustration of a wave of the sea driven and tossed by the wind relates not to insecurity but to instability. All of us are insecure at times and need the reassurance of our God. Having faith does not mean that we never doubt. But it does prompt us to pray, "I do believe. Help me in my unbelief" (see Mark 9:24). Rather than being double-minded, we operate with a singleness of focus on the God we love and serve.

DOING THE WORD

1. What does it mean to ask in faith?
2. How can we be double-minded?

---

1. For greater detail on God's design for prayer, see Stanley D. Gale, *Why Do We Pray?* (Phillipsburg, N.J.: P&R, 2012).

Kindred Spirits

As a flower of the field he will pass away.
—JAMES 1:10

So far, we've been fairly confident in following James's flow of thought. It has been a well-marked trail welcoming believers, in the name of the Lord Jesus Christ, to navigate a difficult path that leads to the blessing of spiritual maturity. For safe conduct on that path, we need the discernment of God's wisdom, which is ours for the asking. Along the way we enjoy a certain delight and expectation from our Father in heaven who set us on the path and walks with us each step of the way.

James has given us tremendous encouragement in the trials we face in life. Our hearts are buoyed to hear that our adversities carry purpose and their level of difficulty is set by God, tailored to our individual need. That knowledge helps us to press on.

But after charting this course, James says something that throws us off balance:

> Let the lowly brother glory in his exaltation,
> but the rich in his humiliation,
> because as a flower of the field he will pass away.
> For no sooner has the sun risen with a burning heat
>   than it withers the grass;
> its flower falls, and its beautiful appearance perishes.
> So the rich man also will fade away in his pursuits.
>   (James 1:9–11)

What does being rich or poor have to do with what James has been describing about handling trials? Evidently, the have-nots of the congregation were being looked down on and even oppressed by those who had.

James will deal with this elephant in the room in detail a bit later. But he introduces the disparity of wealth here to make something perfectly clear—that we all are on the same journey and share the same need. The poor are cut from the same cloth as the rich, and that cloth wears out and fades away.

Whether we walk with our feet shod in two-hundred-dollar sneakers or in two-dollar flip-flops, we all traverse an arduous path in an inhospitable world sharing a common need for wisdom in dealing with the perils and pitfalls of life. When James earlier said, "If any of you lacks wisdom, let him ask of God, who gives to all liberally and without reproach, and it will be given to him" (1:5), the "any" and the "all" of that verse encompass both rich and poor. Having money may help in trials, or it may create its own trials, but no amount of wealth gives anyone greater wherewithal to handle adversity as God wants us to.

Money can be a problem for both rich and poor. It's a problem for the rich because wealth can blind them to their need and lull them into a false sense of security and self-sufficiency. It's a problem for the poor not because they lack riches but because they can buy into the delusion that if they only had money, everything would be okay.

James presents a level playing field and a common need for the wisdom and grace of God. Only through humility are these provisions for the journey received. Humility is what will drive us to ask for wisdom and walk in dependence on our God, as James will later assert: "God resists the proud, but gives grace to the humble" (James 4:6).

DOING THE WORD

1. In what way are we all in the same predicament with the same need?
2. How does James lead all of us to God as our sufficiency?

Chapter 8

Steadfast in Trial

Blessed is the man who endures.

—JAMES 1:12

The radio and internet ads promised huge profits. Hawkers scoffed at piddly returns of 10 percent and urged investors to come to them for the big bucks, at virtually no risk. So described the accounts in the newspaper's exposé of the Ponzi scheme, along with the sad stories of many who had entrusted their life savings to the scam.

Before making any investment, we should do due diligence to examine the product, the claims, and especially who is behind it. James has presented us with an investment option. He has called us to be "all in" in the trials of our lives, telling us that they offer vast dividends for personal investment. No reservation. No doubting. That investment strategy applies to everyone, rich and poor alike. James is urging us to faith in God, believing that He intends our good.

Our approach to trials will depend on our trust in the God who brought them to us. Due diligence calls us to know God and believe His word. Contrary to the "get rich quick" schemes of scammers, the best investments are often long-term. The wisdom is to ride out down times with expectation of better days. James issues the same sort of counsel when he says, "Blessed is the man who remains steadfast under trial" (James 1:12 ESV).

Faith invests in the trials God brings to us. Trials are part of the portfolio of investment vehicles by which our God enriches us in the blessings of salvation. The problem is, though, that trials are the most likely of those vehicles to scare us off because in them we suffer hardship and seeming loss.

That's why James urges us to remain steadfast under trial. Trials are described as tests to be withstood. At worst, we are inclined to resist them. At best, we resign ourselves to them. But our Lord would have us find joy in trials because they prove our faith, build our character, and offer great reward, what James calls "the crown of life which the Lord has promised to those who love Him" (James 1:12).

This crown is not something we merit by our steadfastness. Rather, it represents sharing in the victory of Jesus Christ. Though the crown may adorn our head, we cast it down at the feet of Him who sits on the throne because to Him belong all glory, honor, and praise.

We've heard this language of God's work to those who love Him. Paul uses it in the context of trials in respect to the character of God. He writes to the Romans, "We know that all things work together for good to those who love God" (Rom. 8:28). Paul agrees with James that trials are a source of good and a reason for joy because God is carrying out His workmanship of grace in our lives. Our confidence in trials is found in Him who cannot lie and who keeps His promises.

By knowing God, believing God, and trusting God, faith will persevere in the face of trial. He who began a good work will bring it to completion. We will reap the rewards offered because we trust Him who is faithful to His character and to His word.

DOING THE WORD

1. What keeps you from fully investing in the trials you encounter?
2. What divine dividends does God promise you for steadfastness in faith?

Misreading Trials

Let no one say when he is tempted …

—JAMES 1:13

I can't tell you how many times in my pastoral ministry I have heard someone say, "Why did God allow this to happen?" I have heard it from those young in the faith and from those who had walked with the Lord for many years. Often that question has been a challenge to the goodness of God. Sometimes it has reflected a crisis of faith from someone wondering what sort of God He is and whether He is worthy of trust.

It's not unusual for trials to prompt us to question the character of God. What kind of Father allows His children to endure such hardship? If God is all-powerful, couldn't He have prevented this from happening? These sorts of questions cause us to examine our faith as well. Is my trust misplaced? Have I believed a lie? God promises forgiveness of sins and eternal life, but seeing all these bad things happen, can I be sure?

The value of trials depends on the character of God. Our investment in trials depends on the trustworthiness of God. That's why James goes on to assure us of the character of our God for the profitability of our trials: "Let no one say when he is tempted, 'I am tempted by God'; for God cannot be tempted by evil, nor does He Himself tempt anyone" (James 1:13).

In order for us to grasp James's gist, we need to know that the word for "trial" in the original language has the same linguistic root as the word for "temptation." The word "trials" in verse 2 is the same word translated "temptation" in verse 12 and used as a verb in verse 13. Whether the word is translated "trial" or "temptation" depends on the context, like we might understand the word "green." Context will help us to know whether "green" means color, emotion of envy, environmentally friendly, or a rookie. In this case, James wants us to understand a difference between temptation and trial but also an overlap.

What is James telling us? He is saying that with every trial we face comes temptation. Trials are given to us by God for our good. God does not intend our harm. But present with each trial is the effort of our enemy the devil to lure us to the rocks of spiritual ruin. He seeks to turn us against God, to question His character by asking, "Is God really good?" "Does God really care?" "Is God really able?" "Is God real?"

Perhaps these are questions that have occurred to you. Maybe they have sprung to mind and been quickly repulsed by you. You may have become unnerved that they even occurred to you, maybe even causing you to question your faith.

But these sorts of questions are not blasphemous. They are legitimate questions that arise from your distress of soul in spiritual conflict. Such questions are not to be repressed. They are to be addressed and answered with what God has revealed about Himself in His Word and in His Son. In fact, through the nourishment of God's Word your faith will be strengthened. His truth will be as sandbags holding back the flood of doubt spurred on by our enemy the devil.

DOING THE WORD

1. In what way does every trial from God hold temptation from Satan?
2. How are you to deal with the doubts that besiege you in trials?

Chapter 10

Anatomy of a Seduction

Each one is tempted when …

—JAMES 1:14

Scammers have a variety of techniques to catch our ear, win our trust, and suck us into their schemes. The same is true of Satan, who is at work in our trials not to gain our money but to gain our heart.

James lays out the devil's tactics, which are reminiscent of his approach to Eve in the garden of Eden. There, the devil prompted Eve to question the word of God: "Has God indeed said?" (Gen. 3:1). Then he prompted Eve to question the character of God, suggesting that God was a liar and depriving Eve of what was good. All the while, Satan was appealing to the woman's desire in order to pit her against God and direct her to destruction.

James exposes Satan's tactic to lure us to ruin in our handling trials: "But each one is tempted when he is drawn away by his own desires and enticed. Then, when desire has conceived, it gives birth to sin; and sin, when it is full-grown, brings forth death" (James 1:14–15).

As he did with Eve, the devil appeals to our desires, urging us to make sense of things according to what is right in our own eyes rather than by the word of God. That desire coupled with foolishness resident in our hearts gives birth to sin. Sin yields death. The upshot is that we wither under the heat of trial rather than prosper (see Psalm 1) in God's purpose for us in it.

Knowing our spiritual enemy's intentions and efforts when we face trials, James urges us to clearheaded stalwartness: "Do not be deceived, my beloved brethren" (James 1:16). The term James uses for "deceived" carries the sense of being led astray. Later, James will use the same word when he speaks of wandering from the truth (5:19). A lesson from Eden is that there is danger for us in trials when we depart from the word of God.

Rather than God tempting us in trial, James makes it clear that our Father God is at work for our good: "Every good gift and every perfect gift is from above, and comes down from the Father of lights, with whom there is no variation or shadow of turning" (James 1:17). Our God is the "Father of lights." He is not fickle. He is not temperamental. He does not change like shifting shadows. We can trust Him.

James concludes his thought on God as Father of lights when he says, "Of His own will He brought us forth by the word of truth, that we might be a kind of firstfruits of His creatures" (James 1:18). In other words, He who began a good work in us will bring it to completion. Trials are part of our maturing process in the likeness of Christ. As the writer of Hebrews reminds us, our Father disciplines us as His children for our profit. No discipline "seems to be joyful for the present, but painful; nevertheless, afterward it yields the peaceable fruit of righteousness to those who have been trained by it" (Heb. 12:11).

In trials we need to maintain great vigilance, knowing that our enemy the devil is at work to undermine the purpose of God in them. Our Father is with us, and He has placed us in Christian community to share and bear one another's burdens (see Gal. 6:1–5; Heb. 3:12–13; 10:24–25).

DOING THE WORD

1. What similarities does Satan's temptation of Eve have with his efforts in your trials?
2. How can you combat the devil's effort to undermine God's purposes for you?

Chapter 11

Taking the Reins

Let every man be swift to hear, slow to speak.
—JAMES 1:19

"He hit me first." Have you ever heard that defense from one child who hit another? It's almost as if the violent response was out of the second child's control. But actually, the second child chose to respond in kind to the one who first hit him. Had an authority figure been present, his response may have been quite different.

In the course of our lives, we encounter all sorts of adversity. Some of it is of our own making, but much of it comes to us from the hands of others. But a key consideration in either instance is how we respond. How will we manage ourselves in the midst of a trial? Will our response escalate or deescalate a conflict? Will our actions to manage financial stress exacerbate or alleviate the burden? Will our words enflame or soothe? We find such contrasts in the book of Proverbs: "A soft answer turns away wrath, but a harsh word stirs up anger" (15:1).

The decisive factor in each of these dichotomies rests with us, our actions or reactions. We are the ones who decide between a soft answer or a harsh word. James puts the responsibility squarely on us: "So then, my beloved brethren, let every man be swift to hear, slow to speak, slow to wrath" (James 1:19). In calling us to one course of action, James beckons us away from another. Rather than jumping to conclusions or giving a rash or harsh answer, we are to be measured in how we behave, our actions governed by the lordship of Jesus Christ and ethics of the kingdom to which we belong.

James begins in verse 19 with "so then," an expression of logical connection. But we are left wondering how it connects. James has just written about temptation, and trials before that. How does being quick to hear, slow to speak, and slow to become angry relate to these? Certainly, he is talking about the tongue, a subject he will address later in detail. But here James is talking about our speech in the context of anger. Anger can be a hotbed for sin. When we don't handle anger well, we can give the devil a foothold (Eph. 4:26–27) in our lives.

James is urging us to take caution with our tongues amid the volatility of anger. He urges us to be on guard and to manage ourselves in conflict. Are our actions making us peacemakers or troublemakers? In the few verses we have covered so far, we have seen James emphasize individual responsibility several times in chapter 1: "if any of you" (v. 5), "let him ask" (v. 6), "that man" (v. 7), "the man" (v. 12), "each one" (v. 14), and now "every man" (v. 19).

Our responsibility in any and every situation is to handle it in a manner worthy of our calling in Christ, as we handle ourselves in the wisdom and power that God gives us. Paul urges us to an attitude and ambition of submission to God: "with all lowliness and gentleness, with longsuffering, bearing with one another in love, endeavoring to keep the unity of the Spirit in the bond of peace" (Eph. 4:2–3).

All this brings us to approach trials not as victims but as responsible agents girded with the wisdom and strength of our Lord.

DOING THE WORD

1. How does James empower us to deal with adversity that overtakes us?
2. In whatever trial you are experiencing now, what can you do to handle it?

Chapter 12

Taming the Tongue

Be...slow to wrath; for the wrath of man ...
—JAMES 1:19–20

I remember my grandfather saying, "We don't talk that way in this house." That's exactly what James is saying when he addresses "beloved brethren" (James 1:19). As members of the household of faith, we must control our tongues, guard our speech, and weigh our words. Particularly, James has in mind speech that will contribute to the righteousness God desires. The tongue can tear down, or it can build up.

This is a concern for us because of the danger involved. I had a dachshund with a nasty disposition. We got it from a shelter and it had likely suffered abuse somewhere along the way. He was not friendly, especially around other dogs. We would have to hold tight to his leash lest he launch himself, teeth bared. That awareness and firm grip are what James urges us to when it comes to our tongues, which can be unpredictable and easily provoked.

Our speech is often the weapon of choice in the hands of anger. Whenever we find teaching on anger in the Bible, we find teaching on the tongue in the vicinity. For example, Paul calls us in Ephesians to "be angry, and do not sin" (4:26). A few verses later he teaches on the tongue: "Let no corrupt word proceed out of your mouth, but what is good for necessary edification, that it may impart grace to the hearers" (v. 29). By "corrupt" we might think of harmful, that which is injurious to another.

In giving us a tongue safety course, James does not advocate silence. He is not suggesting we limit our words, although wisdom tells us that "in the multitude of words sin is not lacking, but he who restrains his lips is wise" (Prov. 10:19). James is not addressing the quantity of words, but making sure we use the power of the tongue for good and not for evil, or as Paul put it in Ephesians 4:29, for constructive purposes rather than destructive ones.

Toward that end, James calls for restraint and reflection. Knowing that our tongues in the hand of anger can have hair triggers, we are urged to caution. We should not rush to speak, but be measured in our responses, in keeping with wisdom such as that found in Proverbs 18:13: "He who answers a matter before he hears it, it is folly and shame to him." How many times do we jump to conclusions and spout off an accusation or opinion before we truly understand? It's like those police training simulations where officers are put in volatile situations and end up shooting the little old lady with the dog. Later, James will speak of the tongue being just as deadly. We need to look before we leap, listen before we speak.

When James says we are to be quick to hear, slow to speak, and slow to anger, he is cautioning us about being reactive. It begins with control and intent to listen, listening with an aim to love, or, as Paul expressed it, giving grace (Col. 4:6). Giving grace suggests that even if we do read something right and the other person is in the wrong, we must love them and not treat them as they may deserve. Jesus gives us our example: "When He was reviled, [He] did not revile in return; when He suffered, He did not threaten, but committed Himself to Him who judges righteously" (1 Peter 2:23).

DOING THE WORD

1. In what way is the tongue a weapon in the hand of anger?
2. What power do we find in our words?

The Word on Anger

The wrath of man does not produce the righteousness of God.
—JAMES 1:20

Likely all of us have seen what a war zone looks like: rubble everywhere, the hulking shells of bombed-out buildings, lives decimated, despair palpable. It may take years to build back. Some things can never be recouped. That destruction gives us a glimpse of anger's capability to destroy lives, tear apart relationships, and reduce functioning community to rubble. Recovery from the aftermath of explosion may never fully happen.

James takes this destruction very seriously, particularly when it comes to us being the cause of it. Later, he will speak of the tongue as a fire, a world of unrighteousness (James 3:6), capable of inflicting great damage. Each of us is armed with that incendiary device. That's why James cautions us to "be swift to hear, slow to speak, slow to wrath" (1:19). In other words, we are to be circumspect and exercise great caution in our speech. Words matter.

But James is not only alerting us to danger. He is calling us to devote our speech to what our God wants of us. He points out, "For the wrath of man does not produce the righteousness of God" (James 1:20). So often, our anger is concerned more for our rights than God's righteousness. Often, we react and lash out because what we perceive to be our rights have been trod upon. That parking spot was ours; we saw it first. The promotion should have been ours, not the person who has been at the company two years less than we have.

It may be the case that our anger stems from a motive concerned for the righteousness of God. We get angry at injustice or bullying or even when we see our God blasphemed (see Ps. 139:21–22). This anger is not concerned for us but for others. Even when anger is justified, we are to express it under control and constructively. But more often than not our anger stems from selfish motives when we have been insulted or taken advantage of.

James, however, wants us to remember that the world's ways are not our operating system. We belong to the kingdom of God, which is characterized by righteousness, peace, and joy. We are not to be driven by vainglory but by the glory of God. Our model is the Lord Jesus Christ, as held up by the apostle Paul:

> Let nothing be done through selfish ambition or conceit, but in lowliness of mind let each esteem others better than himself. Let each of you look out not only for his own interests, but also for the interests of others.
>
> Let this mind be in you which was also in Christ Jesus. (Phil. 2:3–5)

How different would our handling of anger be if we adopted the attitude of our Lord Jesus? He did not grasp His rights but relinquished them to the will of His Father. How different would be our handling of trials? So often, our words pour gas on the flames, and the conflagration becomes unmanageable and destructive. We allow our frustrations to boil over or the cancer of bitterness to take root or our rage to control us.

But there is a better way, a way consistent with our calling in Christ, a way of faith that sees and rests and trusts our God. Paul gives us a template for pursuing peace (Rom. 12:9–21), where he highlights use of our tongues and directs us to defer to God. Rather than vengeance, our charge is, "If it is possible, as much as depends on you, live peaceably with all men. Beloved, do not avenge yourselves, but rather give place to wrath; for it is written, 'Vengeance is Mine, I will repay,' says the Lord" (vv. 18–19).

DOING THE WORD

1. In the adversities and conflicts we face, what danger does anger present?
2. How can we pursue righteousness in trials?

Chapter 14

Fruit of the Implanted Word

... brought us forth by the word of truth ...

—JAMES 1:18

Faith makes a radical difference in our lives, at least the faith James is so concerned about helping us understand. Faith is not simply belief in something. Later, James will tell us even the devil has that kind of faith. The faith James has in view testifies to the supernatural intrusion of God in our lives to bring us from spiritual death to spiritual life. With that life come the abilities to know God and to embrace Jesus Christ for salvation. Such faith flows out in newness of life.

How does God communicate this faith to us? He does so by the word of the Holy Spirit regenerating us, causing us to be born again, something our Lord Jesus taught Nicodemus in John 3. In his first letter, Peter describes the outflow of saving faith and its headwaters: "Since you have purified your souls in obeying the truth through the Spirit in sincere love of the brethren, love one another fervently with a pure heart, having been born again, not of corruptible seed but incorruptible, through the word of God which lives and abides forever" (1 Peter 1:22–23).

James mentions these same fruits of genuine faith—obedience, love for God and neighbor, sincerity, fervency, authenticity. James also points us to the same root planted in the soil of God's grace: "Therefore lay aside all filthiness and overflow of wickedness, and receive with meekness the implanted word, which is able to save your souls" (James 1:21). The Holy Spirit works in us through His inspired word, the heart of which is the gospel of Jesus Christ, to cause us to be born again, and through that word cause us to grow in the grace and knowledge of our Lord Jesus.

As new creatures in Christ, we are given dispositions against evil and toward holiness. Peter describes it this way: "As obedient children, not conforming yourselves to the former lusts, as in your ignorance; but as He who called you is holy, you also be holy in all your conduct" (1 Peter 1:14–15). The teaching of Jesus and all the Epistles reflects the Old Testament instruction that the people of God are to live in a manner contrary to the world around us that does not know God. We are a people holy to the Lord.

Consistent with our new life in Christ, James presents us with a negative and a positive, a put off and a put on. We are to put off all filthiness and rampant wickedness because these things are neither consistent with nor appropriate for those now dead to sin and alive in Christ. In addition, we are to put on with humility all that is consistent with new life in Christ. The word implanted in us will take root and bear fruit, as our Lord Jesus put it, thirty, sixty, even a hundredfold (Mark 4:20). True faith will be fruitful, developing in us the character of Christ and producing the good works God has prepared for us to walk in.

The upshot is that whether in tranquility or trial, we are to live in a manner worthy of our calling, looking to honor our Lord, in dependence on the implanted word that animates us.

DOING THE WORD

1. How do we sometimes excuse sin in the heat of trial?
2. How can we cultivate the implanted word in tranquility or in trial?

Chapter 15

Doers of the Word

Be doers of the word, and not hearers only.

—JAMES 1:22

A survey was administered to churchgoers across Christian denominations. One of its questions tried to gauge if sermons really had an impact. The answer was one of those good news/bad news conclusions. The good news was that the vast majority of churchgoers looked forward to the sermon. They found it meaningful and important. The bad news was that those same respondents didn't think the sermon made much difference in their lives.

James would be deeply disturbed by those survey results. Either those people were not paying attention to the word preached, something quite common in our distracted society, or people were not putting into practice what they were hearing.

James holds a high view of the word of God. He has brought our attention so far to the wisdom found in it to navigate our lives to God's glory, including through the tumultuous waters of trials. God uses His word to create life, bringing us forth "by the word of truth" (James 1:18), and to cultivate life through faith in Christ.

James's letter is filled with references to the Holy Scriptures. He speaks of Abraham, Rahab, Job, and Elijah. He draws on them to teach about faith, justification, obedience, perseverance, and prayer. James cites commandments found in Scripture. Clearly, God's written Word is paramount to the believer's perspective and pilgrimage.

Like Jesus, who in the Sermon on the Mount called us to hear His word and put it into practice (Matt. 7:24), James calls us to give ear to our God in His word and to give heed to Him in the conduct of our lives:

"But be doers of the word, and not hearers only, deceiving yourselves" (James 1:22).

It is not sufficient for us to know God's word; we must be practitioners of it. But knowing it is where we must begin. More and more we find ourselves in a biblically illiterate society. More disturbing, we find ourselves in biblically illiterate churches. We don't read the Bible. We don't know what counsel of God to bring to bear in our journey through life, despite the psalmist's declaration, "Your word is a lamp to my feet and a light to my path" (Ps. 119:105). The core of being a disciple of Jesus is being a learner, sitting at His feet to know Him and to know His way.

On hearing the word, we must put it into practice. When James says to "be doers," he is not simply telling us to apply God's word. He is telling us to *become* doers. We are to grow in becoming adept at putting God's counsel into practice. As the writer of Hebrews tells us, "Solid food is for the mature, for those who have their powers of discernment trained by constant practice to distinguish good from evil" (Heb. 5:14 ESV).

Those survey results suggest something is deeply wrong in Christ's church. Believers need to be fortified to contend with the strong currents of cultural godlessness. The same is true for our personal trials. It is through being nourished by a regular diet of God's word and strengthened by its constant practice that we will grow in the fullness of Christ and fulfill His mission for us as His church.

DOING THE WORD

1. Why is doing the word a feature of genuine faith?
2. How can we become doers of the word?

Chapter 16

Deceiving Ourselves

... not hearers only, deceiving yourselves ...

—JAMES 1:22

James cautions us against only hearing God's word and not following through in its application. But he frames being a hearer and not a doer in terms of self-deception: "But be doers of the word, and not hearers only, deceiving yourselves" (James 1:22). The word James uses could also be rendered "deluding." It's a term Paul uses in his letter to the Colossians when he cautions them about being duped by seemingly plausible arguments (Col. 2:4). The expression "deceiving yourselves" puts us on alert because it suggests a possibility or a proclivity for that to happen.

What is James's concern for us when it comes to only being hearers and not doers of the word? His point has to do with presumption. At a vaccination center, people receiving the COVID vaccine were given a colorful sticker that boasted, "I got my COVID-19 vaccine!" I suppose that since it was a sticker, it was intended for display. That sticker attested to people's hearing of the availability and believing in the value of the vaccine and actually getting the shot. They were doers of the word.

But what if someone just walked in and grabbed a sticker? Would owning and displaying it assure them of the vaccine's benefits? No, that would be silly. They would be deceiving themselves and others. And if they counted on that sticker to keep them healthy, they would be deluding themselves as well as misleading others.

That's the way it works with faith. To *say* we believe is no guarantee that we *do* believe. We can be professors of faith without being possessors of it. James's pastoral concern has to do with the genuineness of our faith. Is it real? Is it effective against the mortality of sin? Do we have reason for confidence before God?

James holds out two ways for us to examine our faith for authenticity. One, does it line up with God's word? James will later talk about "faith in our Lord Jesus Christ" (James 2:1 ESV). Faith is not in faith. It is faith in something, trusting our footing, with all that means. Saving faith trusts in Christ alone. Two, does our faith show up in a changed life? James will later tell us that faith without works is dead. Saving faith is receptive to God's word and responsive to it.

When we are not concerned about applying what God says, we "deceive" ourselves. How can we call Jesus "Lord, Lord" and not do what He says? True faith works. It works by taking hold of Christ alone for certain salvation. It works itself out both to will and to do according to the workmanship of God's grace.

Why does James keep hitting this nail of faith on the head? It's because he wants us to take it seriously, to examine ourselves to be sure we are of the household of faith. He also wants us to exercise faith both in trials and in the ordinary course of events that keeps our eyes riveted on Christ our Lord.

DOING THE WORD

1. Why does James lead us to question our faith?
2. How can we combat self-deception?

Chapter 17

Mirror, Mirror, in the Word

He observes himself, goes away, and immediately forgets.

—JAMES 1:24

I heard a story about a congregation's search for a new pastor. Having made it to the final cut, the candidate was brought in for a meet and greet. The get-together involved a picnic and softball game. The candidate stepped up to the plate and hit the ball into the outfield. Rounding first, he slid safely into second base, where he was promptly called out. He protested and became indignant. The congregation got a firsthand view of how this man handled injustices.

That's what trials can do. They bring out the real us, the us hidden to others and even to ourselves. They can expose our idols, accent our unbelief, and showcase what is important to us. Trials are like MRIs to the soul—and that's a good thing through which God can humble us and grow us.

Another way the Spirit gives us insight into ourselves is through the ministry of His word. The Spirit who inspired the Scriptures uses them to expose our hearts. To emphasize this function of the word, James uses the metaphor of a mirror, but with an edge: "For if anyone is a hearer of the word and not a doer, he is like a man observing his natural face in a mirror; for he observes himself, goes away, and immediately forgets what kind of man he was" (James 1:23–24).

Like a regular mirror reflects our external state, the mirror of God's Word reflects the state of our inner being. It certainly shows us our desperate and absolute need for the Savior. When Christians ask, "Mirror, mirror, on the wall, who is the fairest of them all?" the answer will never be us. It will always be fairest Lord Jesus. He alone is without the blemish of sin. He is the image of the invisible God. The mirror of God's Word, illuminated for us by the Holy Spirit, shows us our need for the saving work of Jesus Christ.

The mirror of the Word does something else. It reveals our need for the Savior, but it also reveals how we need to grow in holiness. When the Spirit opens our eyes to something, we are not to neglect it. Rather, we must address it with the wisdom and grace He provides. James speaks of the blessing that accompanies our doing: "But he who looks into the perfect law of liberty and continues in it, and is not a forgetful hearer but a doer of the work, this one will be blessed in what he does" (James 1:25). When we live as our God has designed us, we find contentment, joy, peace, and beauty. We need the grace of our Lord Jesus both for salvation and for sanctification.

James calls the mirror the "law of liberty." When we think of law, we tend to think of restriction, not liberty. Often, we hear that we are to be ourselves, but the law reminds us that we are to be true to what God wants us to be, true to who we are in Christ. We find our spiritual equilibrium and consonance when we live according to who we are in Christ. We might think of a train. When is a train most free—when it bounds derailed across the countryside, or when it speeds along the tracks for which it is designed?

In one sense, we are fully blessed. Our gracious Father has blessed us with *every* spiritual blessing bound up in Jesus Christ that is ours through faith in Him. In another sense, however, we are blessed through walking by faith that looks to Christ and that lives with and for Him. In Jesus, we not only have life, but we also have it abundantly.

DOING THE WORD

1. How can we use the Word of God as a mirror?
2. What is God's purpose for our seeing our reflection in His Word?

Chapter 18

True Religion

This one's religion is useless.

—JAMES 1:26

I came to a saving knowledge of Jesus Christ when I was in college. I had spent my growing years in institutionalized religion that amounted to little more than a label for me. When I moved away from home, I left behind any sort of religious practice and actually became an apologist for atheism to anyone who would engage me. But through involvement with a Christian group on campus, I saw for the first time a religion that flowed from the inside out. Through teaching from the Bible, I learned that I was a sinner and that there was nothing I could do to save myself. And I learned about a savior, *the* Savior, and what He did on my behalf. It was on a brisk October day of my senior year that I walked the campus with my mind racing and my heart burning, returned to my dorm, knelt down by my bed, and embraced God's gift of salvation.

Like many, I gained a disdain for the word "religion." It reminded me of my years of religious ritual and requirements. If you had asked me, I would have said I had faith. But that faith did not rest in Christ alone. It was a faith in my own efforts. For me, religion became a system by which I would earn my way to God's favor. So it gives me pause when I hear James say this: "If anyone among you thinks he is religious, and does not bridle his tongue but deceives his own heart, this one's religion is useless" (James 1:26). What are we to make of James's reference to religion?

"Religion" can be seen as simply a structure of beliefs and practices. It's not good or bad, just descriptive of how Christians or Jews or Muslims exercise the tenets and rituals associated with their belief system. The apostle Paul testified before King Agrippa to his religious practice: "My manner of life from my youth, which was spent from the beginning among my own nation at Jerusalem, all the Jews know. They knew me from the first, if they were willing to testify, that according to the strictest sect of our religion I lived a Pharisee" (Acts 26:4–5). As a Pharisee, Paul practiced his religion differently than would a Sadducee or a Samaritan.

For James, religion speaks of alignment with a belief system and the outworking of it. If we claim to be Christian, what does that look like in our lives? In James's thinking, relationship is not opposed to religion. Rather, relationship shows up in religion. When James speaks of whether our religion is "useless," he has in mind not its effectiveness as a means of salvation but whether the practice of our faith holds value (see 1 Tim. 4:7–10).

Our relationship with Jesus Christ affects our identity, allegiance, priorities, and practices. Such religion involves more than rituals; it reaches to the whole of life. Religion flows from relationship with our Lord Jesus, binding us to Him, holy and called to be holy. Certainly, there are those aspects that are overtly religious, such as attending weekly worship services, but the religion of the believer encompasses all of life for God, with a view to glorify and enjoy Him.

DOING THE WORD

1. What does it mean to be religious?
2. How does being a hearer and doer of the word relate to religion?

Religion before God

Pure and undefiled religion …

—JAMES 1:27

James wants us to think of religion not merely as those formal rituals we do in the practice of our faith but as the exercise of the lordship of Jesus Christ in all of life. That's why he relates religion to bridling the tongue and being both hearers and doers of the word. Our religion has to do with how we treat others and whom we follow. Religion before God springs from a heart occupied by the Holy Spirit and inclined to following Christ. It considers what God requires.

The Pharisees practiced religion, but our Lord Jesus took them to task because theirs was a religion devised by man and devoted to man in the name of God. Note our Lord's assessment:

> Well did Isaiah prophesy of you hypocrites, as it is written:
> "This people honors Me with their lips,
> But their heart is far from Me.
> And in vain they worship Me,
> Teaching as doctrines the commandments of men."
> (Mark 7:6–7)

Jesus gives a scathing review in His litany of pharisaical religious practices that had an appearance of righteousness but were full of hypocrisy and lawlessness (Matt. 23:1–28).

James, however, does not tell us to scrap religion. He tells us of religion before God: "Pure and undefiled religion before God and the Father is this: to visit orphans and widows in their trouble, and to keep oneself unspotted from the world" (James 1:27). Our religion is to reflect the heart of God, what we see throughout the whole Bible.

When he speaks of keeping ourselves unspotted from the world, James is reiterating what he just mentioned as the product of the implanted word, the putting away of moral impurity and wickedness (James 1:21).

The Christian religion is not just a system of doctrine; it is a way of life. As one theologian put it, it is life lived *coram Deo*, before the face of God. More than that, it is life lived for the glory of God who reveals Himself and His will in the pages of Holy Scripture.

Sometimes we hear that the priorities of life for the believer are to put God first, followed by family, work, and self. But that itemized list misses the biblical mark. Priorities are better represented by a wheel that has God at the hub. All of life revolves around Him, is directed by Him, and holds together in Him.

We have seen that in James. The way we regard trials, handle our emotions, and conduct ourselves relates to our relationship with God. Christianity is not relegated to Sunday morning or to prescribed times. It encompasses all of life. The entirety of James's letter can be viewed as an orientation to the Christian religion because it brings the triune God to the fore. Expressions like "word," "faith," "prayer," and "law" are not mere religious jargon; they are the vocabulary of the kingdom of God to which we are alive.

James is calling us to a deeper life than going to church, praying before a meal, or having personal devotions. He calls us to a God-honoring, Christ-serving, Spirit-driven life, where the thoughts and intentions of our hearts and conduct of our lives all seek the God who has claimed us as His own.

DOING THE WORD

1. How have you compartmentalized your life?
2. How does religion relate to your struggles?

Truth Applied

... keep oneself unspotted from the world.

—JAMES 1:27

Sometimes we hear that what we believe is not as important as being sincere in what we believe. That mentality leads to all sorts of problems, many of which are currently dismantling our society. Truth is no longer seen as something objective. What is important is what is true for you or for me. Making matters worse is the imposition of that subjective truth on others and its enforcement by civil and even ecclesiastical government.

James would insist that there is objective truth. That truth is the basis for his teaching. When he speaks of hearing and doing the word, he has in mind the revealed word of God breathed out by the Holy Spirit and recorded in the Bible. When James instructs us to lay aside all wickedness and to keep ourselves unstained from the world, he is calling us to discern between truth and error, right and wrong, good and evil.

Religion before God involves embracing what God has revealed in Scripture, holding fast to it with sincere conviction, and practicing it in our lives. All these are hallmarks of the faith that comes through the work of the Holy Spirit in our hearts.

James calls us to religion that is "pure and undefiled" (James 1:27). The practice of our faith is to be fully in accord with the will of our God, unadulterated by the so-called wisdom of the world, something James will revisit later in his letter. James calls us to hold to an unblemished, uncompromised, wholesome, authentic faith. In a word, we are called to integrity. Integrity carries the dual sense of completeness and consistency. Our doing is to be consistent with our being, which is to be uncorrupted by the state of darkness in which we found ourselves prior to God's regenerating grace. As Paul put it, "For you were once darkness, but now you are light in the Lord. Walk as children of light (for the fruit of the Spirit is in all goodness, righteousness, and truth)" (Eph. 5:8–9).

What does religion before God look like? James spells it out for us in practical terms: "to visit orphans and widows in their trouble, and to keep oneself unspotted from the world" (James 1:27). At first glance, it sounds like James is reducing Christianity to behavior. Yet he is saying nothing different from what our Lord Jesus taught (Matt. 25:34–40) in referring to those who inherit the kingdom prepared for them "from the foundation of the world" (v. 34). Religion before God reflects the heart of God and the priorities of God. Visiting widows, caring for the poor, and living for God in this fallen world are not exhaustive descriptions of the Christian life, but they are reflective of what it means to live for Christ.

True religion before God distinguishes true believers from the unbelieving world that neither knows nor serves Jesus Christ. We are to live unstained from the world, fully consecrated to Christ. Showing mercy, living morally, and embracing truth do nothing to save us. Our salvation is not accomplished by our religion. Rather, it is accomplished by our Redeemer, in whom alone our faith is founded.

DOING THE WORD

1. How does your life reflect the priorities of God and the heart of Christ?
2. Where do you see that you have not kept yourself unblemished from the world?

Chapter 21

The Sin of Partiality

Have you not shown partiality among yourselves, and become judges?

—JAMES 2:4

What would you say are the top three sins you struggle with? Lust? Greed? Anger? James hits on a sin that likely would not even make our top ten. He speaks of the sin of partiality. He appeals to those of the family of faith: "My brethren, do not hold the faith of our Lord Jesus Christ, the Lord of glory, with partiality" (James 2:1). Another translation puts it, "My brothers, show no partiality as you hold the faith in our Lord Jesus Christ, the Lord of glory" (ESV).

What is this sin that slips under the radar for most of us? The idea is showing favoritism based on outward appearance. In contrast, God shows no partiality (Rom. 2:11; Col. 3:25). No one will be treated contrary to his or her due. God is no respecter of persons.

When we hear of partiality, our minds might spring to biases and prejudices like racism, where people are pigeonholed or treated a particular way because of the color of their skin. James, however, speaks to the partiality of position, with particular reference to those who are wealthy.

He paints a picture for us of what such deference might look like:

> For if there should come into your assembly a man with gold rings, in fine apparel, and there should also come in a poor man in filthy clothes, and you pay attention to the one wearing the fine clothes and say to him, "You sit here in a good place," and say to the poor man, "You stand there," or, "Sit here at my footstool." (James 2:2–3)

In other words, we discriminate on the basis of what the world sees of value and extend preferential treatment on that basis. In so doing, we demean and denigrate others. Our love and respect are selective.

The picture James paints is especially egregious because the assembly of which he speaks is the fellowship of the saints, perhaps even an assembly of those gathered for worship. Here God brings us all to a level playing field as debtors to grace, yet we take it on ourselves to discriminate. In so doing, we make artificial distinctions among ourselves "and become judges with evil thoughts" (James 2:4).

James has just explained to us that the religion God wants includes visiting orphans and widows in their affliction. This is consistent with the heart of God for the poor and oppressed. Again, we hear echoes of the Sermon on the Mount, where our Lord described care for the needy but also warned about making a show of it (Matt. 6:1–4). Religion before God reflects His heart but also is conducted for His glory and not our own. So it's no surprise that James would follow up his comments on true religion with mention of the poor.

But James has something even more basic in view—the gospel itself. Faith in our Lord Jesus Christ is for *all* who believe. Just as all have sinned, by grace all God has chosen (James 2:5) will be counted righteous through faith in Christ. In that sense we are all poor, without means to commend ourselves to God, without recourse to save ourselves. The only partiality we are to show is to Christ as Lord, recognizing Him as Lord and ourselves as His servants.

DOING THE WORD

1. In what ways are you inclined to consider yourself better than others?
2. Why is partiality a sin against God and neighbor?

Chapter 22

Rich in Faith

... rich in faith and heirs of the kingdom ...

—JAMES 2:5

Our Lord Jesus gives a lesson in kingdom economics in Luke's gospel account. He describes the thought process of a wealthy man. The man possessed an abundance of goods, but he had a problem. He didn't have room for his increasing crops. His solution was not to give away his goods, sharing them with the poor. Instead, he came up with a different approach. Jesus tells us of his plan: "I will do this: I will pull down my barns and build greater, and there I will store all my crops and my goods. And I will say to my soul, 'Soul, you have many goods laid up for many years; take your ease; eat, drink, and be merry'" (Luke 12:18–19). Jesus made clear how foolhardy that investment scheme was since God could take it all from him in an instant. Our Lord gives us the bottom line when He says, "So is he who lays up treasure for himself, and is not rich toward God" (v. 21).

Economics of the kingdom of God run counter to those of the kingdom of this world and should radically affect our perspective and attitude. It is so easy to look down on others, for whatever reason. When it comes to wealth, we can look down on both rich and poor. We can regard with contempt those who are rich because they spend money on what we deem exorbitance. We can demean in our sight those who are poor because we consider them below our station. In both cases, we adopt the self-righteous position of the Pharisee that we are better than others (Luke 18:11).

All sin of partiality neglects the perspective given by the apostle Paul: "What do you have that you did not receive? Now if you did indeed receive it, why do you boast as if you had not received it?" (1 Cor. 4:7). And in keeping with our Lord's parable, if we did receive it, we are to honor the Lord who gave it to us. James presents the prospectus of kingdom gain: "Listen, my beloved brethren: Has God not chosen the poor of this world to be rich in faith and heirs of the kingdom which He promised to those who love Him?" (James 2:5).

Contrary to the ways of this world, James says it is the poor God has chosen to be rich in faith. It is not that their poverty qualifies them for the kingdom, but that God's ways are not our ways. We see that exhibited in the grace of Christ: "For you know the grace of our Lord Jesus Christ, that though He was rich, yet for your sakes He became poor, that you through His poverty might become rich" (2 Cor. 8:9).

Evidently, the people were enamored with wealth and gave special deference to the rich, but James gives them a dose of realism: "Do not the rich oppress you and drag you into the courts? Do they not blaspheme that noble name by which you are called?" (James 2:6–7).

James presents the sin of partiality as an affront to the gospel. If we hold to the faith in our Lord Jesus, the Lord of glory who humbled Himself, we cannot help but see ourselves as debtors to the unmerited, unexpected, undeserving favor of our God. Our position of privilege has nothing to do with who we are or what we have. It has everything to do with the love of God conditioned only on His sovereign, saving purpose. If we have little, we want to receive it with gratitude and exercise stewardship of it for the kingdom of God. If we have much, we want to receive it with gratitude and exercise stewardship of it for the kingdom of God.

DOING THE WORD

1. How can we be rich toward God?
2. How does the humility of indebtedness affect our attitude toward others?

Chapter 23

The Royal Law

Fulfill the royal law according to the Scripture.
—JAMES 2:8

James has just addressed the sin of partiality. People were discriminating against one another on the basis of status, something out of accord with Christlike character. Partiality, however, was illustrative of a greater principle, what James calls "the royal law": "If you really fulfill the royal law according to the Scripture, 'You shall love your neighbor as yourself,' you do well; but if you show partiality, you commit sin, and are convicted by the law as transgressors" (James 2:8–9).

For James, partiality is the sin of not loving your neighbor as yourself. It is a violation of the second great commandment (Matt. 22:39) and a transgression of God's standard for relating to others. Would we want to be treated as inferior to others? Certainly not! Then we should do unto others as we would have them do unto us.

Sometimes we set law and love against one another. Perhaps we think of love being more permissive and the law more prescriptive. Or, as a friend of mine thought, perhaps law is Old Testament; love is New Testament. But in the Bible, there is no tension between the two. Our Lord Jesus summarized the law in terms of love, love for God and love for neighbor (Matt. 22:36–40). Both of these commandments are found in the Old Testament. The commandment to love God in Deuteronomy 6 follows the giving of the law in Deuteronomy 5. The commandment to love neighbor is found in Leviticus 19:18.

James calls the second great commandment "the royal law." Why do you suppose he labels it "royal"? Likely because it is associated with the character of our King and conduct in His kingdom, a rule just referenced by James: "Listen, my beloved brethren: Has God not chosen the poor of this world to be rich in faith and heirs of the kingdom which He promised to those who love Him?" (James 2:5).

Love for others, whether brethren or neighbor, is a hallmark of the kingdom of God and characteristic of the King we serve. We who are subjects and heirs of that kingdom are to display such love. Negatively, that means we are to refrain from sins like partiality that hold a standard contrary to the grace we have received. Positively, we are to consider how we would like to be treated as a measure for how we treat others.

Keeping the royal law is living out the gospel of our Lord Jesus Christ. The gospel does not just have to do with forgiveness of sin and eternal life. As Jesus put it, it is the gospel *of the kingdom* (Matt. 4:23; 9:35; emphasis added). The good news of our freedom in Christ has bearing on both our status and our service. We live in respect to our King.

James speaks not only of keeping the royal law but also of fulfilling it. The word "fulfill" (James 2:8) caries the sense of goal, like we would fulfill the purpose of being sent on an errand by coming back with what was requested of us. Love is the charter of the kingdom of God and represents God's ambition for us in relating to others.

What will people see when we exhibit this love? They will not see arrogance, rudeness, selfishness, judgmentalism, or gossip. Instead, reflecting our King, they will witness patience, kindness, humility, sacrifice, and forgiveness. They will see Christ in us, the hope of glory.

DOING THE WORD

1. In what way is the law the teeth of love for God and neighbor?
2. What does it mean to love our neighbor as ourselves?

Chapter 24

The Law of Liberty

Do as those who will be judged by the law of liberty.
—JAMES 2:12

Our Lord Jesus lays out a purpose statement for us who have been brought to bow the knee before Him as Savior and Lord. He tells us in the Sermon on the Mount to "seek first the kingdom of God and His righteousness" (Matt. 6:33). That directive applies to whatever situation in which we find ourselves, whether adversity or prosperity. Each circumstance holds its own peculiar challenges in keeping Christ at the fore.

Seeking God's kingdom involves perspective and practice, how we look at life and how we handle life. Christ is on the throne of our hearts, and every aspect of our lives is to reflect that lordship, hearing His word and putting it into practice.

James has just called us to love our neighbors as ourselves, echoing what our Lord Jesus taught. We find many parallels between Christ's teaching and what James drives home in his letter, including the three reasons he appends to living out the royal law. Each of these reasons is marked by the same conjunction of logic ("for").

First, the royal law does not allow for selective obedience: "For whoever shall keep the whole law, and yet stumble in one point, he is guilty of all" (James 2:10). James is not suggesting we can save ourselves. If anything, he is pointing out the impossibility of it. We look in the mirror of God's law, and we see sinners in absolute need of a savior. Rather, James is calling us to kingdom righteousness. As Jesus put it, "You shall be perfect, just as your Father in heaven is perfect" (Matt. 5:48).

Second, the royal law is not some impersonal statute but reflects the character of the God whose law it is and the kingdom into which He has delivered us. "For He who said, 'Do not commit adultery,' also said, 'Do not murder.' Now if you do not commit adultery, but you do murder, you have become a transgressor of the law. So speak and so do as those who will be judged by the law of liberty" (James 2:11–12).

Here James picks up on language he used earlier, the "law of liberty" (see James 1:25). Liberty does not suggest lawlessness but a love-motivated compliance. As our Lord put it, "If you love Me, keep My commandments" (John 14:15). Obedience expresses allegiance in the outflow of relationship.

The final reason marked by James's conjunction of logic for keeping the royal law is a symptom of salvation, evidence of saving faith. "For judgment is without mercy to the one who has shown no mercy. Mercy triumphs over judgment" (James 2:13). If the royal law is loving our neighbor as ourselves, we can ask ourselves, "Would I want judgment or mercy if I did wrong?" We see this reasoning in the Old Testament context for loving others: "You shall not take vengeance, nor bear any grudge against the children of your people, but you shall love your neighbor as yourself: I am the LORD" (Lev. 19:18). Just as we would not take vengeance on ourselves, so love mandates mercy.

DOING THE WORD

1. How does each of the three reasons for fulfilling the royal law relate to loving others?
2. How does God enable you to love in this way?

Chapter 25

Faith Plus Works?

... if someone says he has faith but does not have works.

—JAMES 2:14

In turning to the second half of James 2, we find what some consider a notorious teaching: "You see then that a man is justified by works, and not by faith only" (v. 24). This teaching prompted Martin Luther to declare James "an epistle of straw" and to question its inclusion in the New Testament.

Surely, here we have found a contradiction in Scripture, one that reaches to the heart of the gospel itself. After all, didn't Paul insist that "therefore ... a man is justified by faith apart from the deeds of the law" (Rom. 3:28)? As the "therefore" indicates, Paul arrived at that conclusion after a careful explanation of righteousness not being found through our obedience to the law but through faith in Christ's obedience to the law. As sinners, we are incapable of the obedience God requires. God provided that spotless righteousness through Christ.

No wonder Luther reacted so strongly to James's assertion. To add works to faith as a basis for justification before God would have undermined the newfound assurance he had come to understand through his study of the book of Romans.

Interestingly, both James and Paul appeal to Abraham to make their point. On the one hand, James says, "Was not Abraham our father justified by works when he offered Isaac his son on the altar?" (James 2:21). Paul, on the other hand, asserts, "If Abraham was justified by works, he has something to boast about, but not before God. For what does the Scripture say? 'Abraham believed God, and it was accounted to him for righteousness'" (Rom. 4:2–3). Will the real Abraham please stand up? Or more to the point, will the real gospel please stand out? How are we saved?

The single, unified, unadulterated testimony of Scripture is that our salvation is accomplished by God through the work of His Son. Paul, in particular, drives home that we are saved by grace alone, through faith alone, in Christ alone. By way of personal testimony, he makes it clear that any religious credential or merit he had accrued was worthless for his acceptance before God (Phil. 3:4–9). By way of theological explanation, Paul is careful to point to Christ:

> But when the kindness and the love of God our Savior toward man appeared, not by works of righteousness which we have done, but according to His mercy He saved us, through the washing of regeneration and renewing of the Holy Spirit, whom He poured out on us abundantly through Jesus Christ our Savior, that having been justified by His grace we should become heirs according to the hope of eternal life. (Titus 3:4–7)

But Paul has more to say. The grace that saves is the grace that sanctifies, growing us in Christlikeness:

> For the grace of God that brings salvation has appeared to all men, teaching us that, denying ungodliness and worldly lusts, we should live soberly, righteously, and godly in the present age, looking for the blessed hope and glorious appearing of our great God and Savior Jesus Christ, who gave Himself for us, that He might redeem us from every lawless deed and purify for Himself His own special people, zealous for good works. (Titus 2:11–14)

It is this fruit of faith to which James points. We are saved by faith alone, but not by faith that is alone. Like a seed, the gospel flowers in beauty with the fruit of works fragrant with the scent of grace.

DOING THE WORD

1. What does it mean to say we are saved by faith alone but not by faith that is alone?
2. What assurance does a godly inclination in your life give you?

Working Faith

Faith by itself, if it does not have works, is dead.

—JAMES 2:17

James asks the hard questions about faith. In our day, it is poor form to question someone's faith. After all, we're talking about something subjective and personal. Questioning faith would be like questioning someone's favorite color.

James, however, has a more pastoral concern in mind. He doesn't want someone investing in a scam. Or put differently, he doesn't want anyone appearing before the judgment seat of God to hear the words, "I never knew you; depart from Me, you who practice lawlessness!" (Matt. 7:23). Rather, he wants to ensure that we hear our Lord say, "Well done, good and faithful servant; you have been faithful over a few things, I will make you ruler over many things. Enter into the joy of your lord" (25:23; see also v. 34). Which reception we are given hinges on the nature of our faith.

Just because people are sincere or confident does not mean their faith is authentic. Like we might push a test button on a smoke alarm, James gives us a way to examine our faith to see if indeed it is not dead but alive with the power of God:

> What does it profit, my brethren, if someone says he has faith but does not have works? Can faith save him? If a brother or sister is naked and destitute of daily food, and one of you says to them, "Depart in peace, be warmed and filled," but you do not give them the things which are needed for the body, what does it profit? (James 2:14–16)

James is simply reiterating what our Lord Jesus taught when He described the visible faith of those chosen from the foundation of the world (Matt. 25:34–40).

James says merely a claim of faith is not enough. It is subject to scrutiny. How can we scrutinize the unseen? We test the genuineness of faith by seeing if it flows out in kingdom behavior.

If we claim to have faith but don't see evidence, we can conclude that that "faith" is dead (James 2:17). It will not save from condemnation. It is not true faith that justifies but spurious faith without hope and without God.

Sometimes when we talk about clothing and feeding the poor, we are accused of holding to a social gospel that looks to social justice and physical needs rather than to the salvation of the soul. But consistent with the preaching of Jesus, James says that genuine faith shows up in a love for others, and that love is not in word only but in deed as well.

The works of which James speaks do not commend us to God or contribute to the work of Christ. Rather, they serve as commentary on the nature and health of the faith we profess. As Paul put it, saving faith is a gift of God (Eph. 2:8–9), and that faith and its works reflect God's workmanship (v. 10).

DOING THE WORD

1. How is faith related to works?
2. What pastoral concern is James expressing in explaining saving faith?

Chapter 27

A Question of Faith

You have faith, and I have works.

—JAMES 2:18

Sometimes the way a question is framed makes it impossible to answer directly. Perhaps you've heard someone pit the love of God against His justice. "Is God a God of wrath and justice, or a God of love and mercy?" they will press you. But we cannot answer that question as it is presented. Scripture explains to us that God is both just and merciful. These attributes of God coalesce at the cross, as illustrated in John's Gospel: "For God so loved the world that He gave His only begotten Son, that whoever believes in Him should not perish but have everlasting life" (John 3:16). The love of God rises in splendor against the dark backdrop of His justice. Remove the wrath ("perish"), and the love loses its splendor.

James takes a similar approach for those who would try to set faith and works in opposition. "But someone will say, 'You have faith, and I have works.' Show me your faith without your works, and I will show you my faith by my works" (James 2:18). Rather than pitting faith and works against each other, James describes the relationship between the two.

When James says, "Show me," he is acting like a physician. When we go to the doctor for a sick visit, the doctor will ask us a series of probing questions and conduct some diagnostic tests. That examination will enable the physician to conclude what is probably going on with us. That conclusion is a diagnosis, from which treatment will be prescribed.

That is the relationship James wants us to understand between faith and works. It's true that our efforts have no bearing in our salvation, as Paul makes abundantly clear (Gal. 2:16). Our works do not factor in to our standing before God. Only Christ's works have merit, and we receive His works on our behalf by grace through faith.

James, however, teaches that our works do have a place. They are evidence of God's handiwork of grace in our lives. They are symptoms of a new heart, of genuine faith, and of the presence of the Holy Spirit in our lives uniting us to Jesus Christ. Faith animates the works we do, and faith compels those works because we are alive in Christ. James makes it clear that saving faith cannot be asymptomatic (James 2:20). It must and will evidence itself.

As a pastor, I had the privilege and delight with the elders of the church serving alongside me to examine those who presented themselves for membership. We had the responsibility before God of assessing whether those who were professors of faith were in actuality possessors of it. How did we do that? We didn't have a spiritual x-ray machine. Rather, we had to rely on symptoms of faith.

Saving faith shows itself in what it does and what it says. A testimony would have to involve more than spouting off religious doctrine. James points out that even Satan has correct knowledge of who Jesus is and what He has done (James 2:19). Did those seeking membership acknowledge their sin, forsake any ability to commend themselves to God, and trust in Christ alone for salvation? Moreover, did their lives reflect the lordship of Jesus Christ as they sought to obey and serve Him? That's where works come to bear, not as a résumé of righteous deeds but as compulsion of loving, lively faith in Jesus Christ.

DOING THE WORD

1. Why is mere accurate belief insufficient for salvation?
2. What are some symptoms of saving faith?

Chapter 28

Functional Faith

Faith without works is dead.

—JAMES 2:26

It's one thing to be told how to do something; it's quite another to be shown how to do it. When I have to make a repair to my car, I can often find step-by-step directions in the owner's manual. Much more helpful to me is searching for the specific repair online and finding a video that walks me through it. To help us form a proper conception of faith, James holds up two figures from the Old Testament to illustrate.

James begins with Abraham:

> Was not Abraham our father justified by works when he offered Isaac his son on the altar? Do you see that faith was working together with his works, and by works faith was made perfect? And the Scripture was fulfilled which says, "Abraham believed God, and it was accounted to him for righteousness." And he was called the friend of God. You see then that a man is justified by works, and not by faith only. (James 2:21–25)

At first glance, we are surprised to see James using Abraham as an example of a man justified by works. After all, didn't Paul use Abraham to teach the opposite? "For if Abraham was justified by works, he has something to boast about, but not before God. For what does the Scripture say? 'Abraham believed God, and it was accounted to him for righteousness'" (Rom. 4:2–3). Paul goes on to explain in detail that justification is by faith, not by works. But James wants to see that the faith Paul talks about flows out in works. In other words, Abraham exercised the obedience of faith.

Next, James holds up for us the Old Testament figure of Rahab: "Likewise, was not Rahab the harlot also justified by works when she received the messengers and sent them out another way?" (James 2:25). Faith was at work in Rahab, as was the case with Abraham. Both figures serve as illustrations for us of what faith looks like.

In these two figures, James wants us to see a functional faith, a faith that shows itself in practical ways. These two, both featured in the hall of faith in Hebrews 11, represent two extremes: a male and a female, a prominent figure and a peripheral figure, a respected person and one not so much, a Jew and a Gentile. James makes the contrast stark when he describes each: "Abraham our father" and "Rahab the harlot."

In both examples God's workmanship manifests itself similarly. Faith is inclined toward God, believing what He says, entrusting itself to His will, and acting in obedience. The faith of Abraham was not a different species from the faith of Rahab. There are no degrees of saving faith. Faith is authentic or inauthentic, alive or dead. That is the conclusion James wants us to understand: "For as the body without the spirit is dead, so faith without works is dead also" (James 2:26).

James has labored hard to make sure we understand faith that saves (James 2:14). He has explained it to us, illustrated it for us, and provided examples for us to see what it looks like. In so doing, James wants us to take stock of our own profession of faith. His pastoral heart is in play, making sure we are not fooling ourselves with some knockoff faith that can never save. He also wants us to understand that our faith looks to God as its author for navigating the choppy seas of the Christian life.

DOING THE WORD

1. How do Abraham and Rahab illustrate faith for us?
2. What confidence do we find in lively faith?

Chapter 29

Careless Words

We all stumble in many things.

—JAMES 3:2

James has already touched on the topic of the tongue. In chapter 1 of his letter, he urged us to be "swift to hear, slow to speak, slow to wrath" (v. 19). There we saw that our words are the weapon of choice in the hand of anger. At the close of chapter 1, James describes true religion in terms of bridling the tongue. The religious tongue is not one of lip service that talks a good talk, but the expression of true faith consecrated to Jesus Christ. In these passages we've gotten a feel for the power of our words, both to help and to harm.

In chapter 3 James returns to the tongue, where he gives us a fuller picture of its potential. Over half of the chapter deals with the subject, coming at it from a variety of directions and with a mixture of metaphors. With this fuller picture comes a dire word of caution. It's like those triangular warning signs on the back of tanker trucks: "DANGER! Highly Flammable." Those trucks carry fuel, ordinary and necessary for the routine of everyday life but capable of great danger and labeled for all to know.

It's curious how James broaches the subject of the tongue. He begins with an application before he launches into an analysis: "My brethren, let not many of you become teachers, knowing that we shall receive a stricter judgment. For we all stumble in many things. If anyone does not stumble in word, he is a perfect man, able also to bridle the whole body" (James 3:1–2).

He begins not by talking about the tongue as a weapon but by addressing an occupation that uses the tongue as a basic tool—a teacher. Then, by way of the conjunction "for," he notes that all of us (not just teachers) "stumble" in what we say. The idea is that we sin because our tongue trips us up.

The capacity of the tongue to hurt others resides with each of us because we all have words at our disposal, whether those words are tools of our trade or avenues of communication in our households or language for interactions with those we meet. Each word, improperly placed, can be a bomb to a relationship and inflict serious injury to others and bring dishonor to our Lord. No wonder the psalmist prays, "Set a guard, O LORD, over my mouth; keep watch over the door of my lips" (Ps. 141:3).

This entire take on the tongue in James 3:1–12 is couched in the negative. James casts it as an incendiary device, a deadly poison, a restless evil, a world of unrighteousness. Why does James speak in such strong negative terms? For the same reason parents tell their kids not to play with matches. The potential for harm is real and not to be toyed with.

James's word to us about the tongue is always timely, but it carries another application in our day. We can throw words around so carelessly on social media. Much like a soldier lobs a grenade, we can blow up a comment thread with negative speech. Because we are people of faith, our words must honor our Lord and look to build up others. By what we contribute to a conversation, we act as de facto teachers, giving counsel that reflects the royal law — or not.

DOING THE WORD

1. What does James mean when he speaks of your tongue?
2. In what way are you a teacher through your words?

Chapter 30

Brash Words

The tongue is a little member and boasts great things.
—JAMES 3:5

When I was growing up, Saturday mornings were cartoon time. I assumed my role as couch potato and gave myself over to the mind-numbing world of animation. Tom, Jerry, the Jetsons, Snagglepuss, Quickdraw McGraw, the Roadrunner, and others became familiar friends. One friend in particular was a pint-sized powerhouse named Mighty Mouse. With the abilities of Superman, the flying rodent would swoop in to save the day.

James alerts us to another powerful diminutive denizen that we would be foolish to disregard. In chapter 1, he urged us to bridle the tongue. Now, in chapter 3, James warns us to make sure that bridle is secure because if the tongue is not held in check, it can do exceeding damage.

James illustrates the power of the tongue by comparing it to something small that controls something large. "Indeed, we put bits in horses' mouths that they may obey us, and we turn their whole body. Look also at ships: although they are so large and are driven by fierce winds, they are turned by a very small rudder wherever the pilot desires" (James 3:3–4). Just think, your capacity to speak can have great significance and lasting consequence on others, beginning with those closest to you. Your words can build up or tear down, set the tone and plot the course. As the rudder serves the will of the boat pilot, we need to be intentional in our speech and circumspect in our conversation. Our hands must be firmly on the reins.

The untamed tongue is particularly prone to boasting: "Even so the tongue is a little member and boasts great things. See how great a forest a little fire kindles!" (James 3:5). Why would James identify boasting as the incendiary device in the explosiveness of the tongue? How does boasting contribute to the volatility of our speech? James helps us when he analyzes the components of boasting: "But if you have bitter envy and self-seeking in your hearts, do not boast and lie against the truth" (James 3:14). We'll address this text in another devotion, but for now we can see the explosive charge resident in our tongues, which is the self-centered, self-serving, destructive nature of self-glory.

Reaching a bit deeper in our analysis, we find that at the heart of boasting is pride. The boasting of the tongue exalts self. Even more serious, it exalts self at the expense of God. Notice the line in the sand drawn by the psalmist:

> May the LORD cut off all flattering lips,
> And the tongue that speaks proud things,
> Who have said,
> "With our tongue we will prevail;
> Our lips are our own;
> Who is lord over us?" (Ps. 12:3–4)

Boasting reflects self-service and self-sufficiency. Boasting is "evil" (James 4:16; see vv. 13–16) in that it usurps the glory and prerogative that belong only to God (Prov. 27:1). That's why James will say shortly, "God resists the proud, but gives grace to the humble" (James 4:6).

When James highlights the tongue boasting great things, he has more in mind than tooting our own horn. He has in mind our adopting a posture that sets ourselves up as a rival to God, to whom alone belongs all glory, honor, and praise. Guarding our tongues reaches to more than our words.

DOING THE WORD

1. What does the motive behind your words say about your heart before God?
2. Why does James draw attention to the size of the tongue?

Chapter 31

Kingdom Caution

The tongue is a fire, a world of iniquity.

—JAMES 3:6

In the state of California, 2020 was a record-setting year for wildfires. Almost ten thousand fires burned over four million acres of land, destroying homes and structures to the tune of ten billion dollars in property damage. A Cal Fire website claims that "approximately 95% of all wildfires in California are caused by human activity." This generated the "One Less Spark—One Less Wildfire" campaign, instructing people in how to prevent wildfires.

James expresses the same concern when it comes to the tongue, with potentially far more serious implications:

> Even so the tongue is a little member and boasts great things.
>
> See how great a forest a little fire kindles! And the tongue is a fire, a world of iniquity. The tongue is so set among our members that it defiles the whole body, and sets on fire the course of nature; and it is set on fire by hell. (James 3:5–6)

Forest fires can damage property and even take lives. But the tongue can inflict devastation on hearts and relationships.

James makes sure we understand the capability of our words. He describes the tongue as "a fire, a world of iniquity" and "an unruly evil, full of deadly poison" (James 3:8), stoked by nothing less than the fires of hell. The words we speak can convey heaven or hell. Paul lays out a user's manual for the tongue, along with warnings similar to James:

> Let no corrupt word proceed out of your mouth, but what is good for necessary edification, that it may impart grace

> to the hearers. And do not grieve the Holy Spirit of God, by whom you were sealed for the day of redemption. Let all bitterness, wrath, anger, clamor, and evil speaking be put away from you, with all malice. And be kind to one another, tenderhearted, forgiving one another, even as God in Christ forgave you. (Eph. 4:29–32)

We've noted that the book of James is New Testament Wisdom Literature and that it holds many parallels to Christ's Sermon on the Mount. There, our Lord Jesus also connects our words with the fire of hell: "But I say to you that whoever is angry with his brother without a cause shall be in danger of the judgment. And whoever says to his brother, 'Raca!' shall be in danger of the council. But whoever says, 'You fool!' shall be in danger of hell fire" (Matt. 5:22). Like a scalpel in the hands of a skilled surgeon, our words hold great power and great potential in the hand of wisdom calibrated to the fear of the Lord.

What we see in the tongue (*our* tongue) is the potential for widespread destruction, more in keeping with the kingdom of the evil one than the kingdom of righteousness, joy, and peace we belong to and represent. James warns us that a careless word can be the spark to great devastation, like a forest can be decimated by the conflagration created by an errant ember.

James says this fire starter resides in each of us and can affect the whole body, both individually and the community in which we live and move for Christ. By the grace of God, we can harness this awesome power for good and not for evil, to build up not to tear down, to point others to Christ, our King.

DOING THE WORD

1. What warning for our words does James issue?
2. What would be part of a tongue safety course?

Chapter 32

Domesticating the Tongue

No man can tame the tongue.

—JAMES 3:8

My seminary curriculum required me to learn Hebrew and Greek so that I could study the Bible in its original languages. Part of that study involved memorizing vocabulary. To help me I would use mnemonic devices like word association. For example, a Hebrew word for "forgive" is *nasa.'* I would associate with this Hebrew word the acronym NASA (National Aeronautics and Space Administration) and think that forgiving the sin of another is like launching a rocket into space, separating the sinner from the sin. My trick for remembering the Hebrew word for tongue, *lashon*, involved relating it to a "tongue lashing," a severe scourging with words.

We can employ the same mnemonic to understand the lesson James has for us regarding the tongue. We can use our speech to lash out at someone, or we can keep it restrained on a leash. One thing is for certain, though: we can never let our tongue run wild: "For every kind of beast and bird, of reptile and creature of the sea, is tamed and has been tamed by mankind. But no man can tame the tongue. It is an unruly evil, full of deadly poison" (James 3:7–8).

Some people are not satisfied with having a cat or dog as a pet. They want something more unusual. Some have befriended a wolf or a bobcat from birth. They show pictures of these animals snuggling and being nonthreatening, just part of the family. The problem is these animals retain their wild disposition and are unpredictable. Unguarded, they can strike out with horrific consequences. So it is with our tongues. They cannot be tamed and so must be guarded and restrained.

James, however, speaks of more than restraint when it comes to our speech. He notes the potential of the tongue to generate both blessing and cursing: "With it we bless our God and Father, and with it we curse men, who have been made in the similitude of God. Out of the same mouth proceed blessing and cursing. My brethren, these things ought not to be so" (James 3:9–10).

James saying "ought" means that we can view our words as appropriate or inappropriate. We who belong to God, who are subjects of His kingdom, have no business conducting ourselves like those who do not know Jesus Christ. There is appropriate speech for us, and there is inappropriate speech. As we saw previously, our words are not to tear down but to build up (Eph. 4:29) because we are indwelt by the Holy Spirit and bear the name of Christ. Just as sexual immorality and covetousness are improper for us as children of God, so crude joking is inappropriate (Eph. 5:3–4). Why? Because we are to reflect the character of our God and walk in love (vv. 1–2). Our position in Christ is to govern everything about us.

In addition, who are *we* to look down on or curse others? They are image bearers of God just as we are. We are to afford them the same honor and respect as we would want for ourselves. Again, we hear echoes of the royal law. We have standing before God not because of anything great about us, but only because of God's grace.

James is calling on us to manage our tongues according to righteousness. If we belong to the kingdom of God, having hearts brought to bow before the Lord Jesus Christ, then we must direct our tongues toward righteousness and peace. Our tongues are not to be attack dogs protecting our own domain but are to be service dogs for loving God and neighbor.

DOING THE WORD

1. Why does God care about your words?
2. How can our words relate to seeking first the kingdom of God and His righteousness?

Chapter 33

Window on Wisdom

Works are done in the meekness of wisdom.
—JAMES 3:13

I live about twenty minutes from Longwood Gardens, sprawling botanical grounds that cover over a thousand acres. Between the Terrace Restaurant and the Conservatory, there's significant construction going on to improve and expand the visitor experience. You can hear the roar of heavy equipment moving the earth out of the way in service to the construction plans. They have a big wall set up around the area to keep the public out and to allow the equipment its space to maneuver. In that wall, they have placed windows so that people can look in and see all that's going on as the project takes shape.

That's what James does as he again turns to the topic of wisdom. He says our hearts are loud with the sound of activity. The construction crew of wisdom is at work, busy with the building project of our lives. James calls us over to the window to peer in. And what he directs our attention to is not just all the heavy equipment rumbling around. He calls our attention to the manufacturer of the machinery to give us an idea of what is taking shape. He begins with a question that captures our attention, beckoning us over to the window of our hearts: "Who is wise and understanding among you? Let him show by good conduct that his works are done in the meekness of wisdom" (James 3:13).

In taking up the topic of wisdom once again, James particularly wants to warn of counterfeit wisdom, wisdom that appears competent for the job but will actually accomplish destruction rather than construction. James has already warned us of what happens when we misread a situation or misjudge God (James 1:13–15). Behind the effort to mislead us is our spiritual adversary the devil. James will give us a more explicit explanation and direction in chapter 4, when he speaks of resisting the devil. But here, in dealing with wisdom, he urges us to great caution and careful examination of what exactly is on the worksite of our hearts. James tells us to be on guard against a wisdom that is not from above, which he describes as "earthly, sensual, demonic" (3:15).

As we saw in chapter 1, wisdom that is consistent with genuine faith comes from God, looks at life from the perspective of God, lives life God's way, and serves God's ends. Wisdom involves a Godward life. Like the flower that bends toward the light of the sun, wisdom causes us to lift our faces to our God. This is why James says wisdom that is the real deal will show up in character and behavior marked by it.

Strangely, James speaks of the "meekness of wisdom" (James 3:13). We might expect "strength of wisdom" or "skill of wisdom." Why meekness? Meekness is associated with humility, a key characteristic for kingdom life and for the conduct of spiritual warfare that is part of the ordinary Christian experience. Such wisdom always adopts the posture of a subcontractor, deferring to God, serving His ends, following His blueprint.

When James asks, "Who is wise and understanding among you?" (James 3:13), he takes us each aside and presses on us personal responsibility. He calls us to take stock, to examine ourselves, and to make needed corrections in thought and action.

DOING THE WORD

1. Why do we need to be circumspect about how we are growing spiritually?
2. How does wisdom relate to conduct?

Chapter 34

Demonic Wisdom

This wisdom does not descend from above.
—JAMES 3:15

Like "jumbo shrimp," "demonic wisdom" presents a contradiction. Wisdom, after all, is associated with the fear of the Lord. If any word would be connected to demons, it would be "folly" or "wickedness." James, however, speaks of wisdom that is demonic because it has the appearance of wisdom. It presents the way that seems right but is, in fact, the way of death, just like in the garden of Eden when the serpent drew near to reason together with Eve. The devil impugned the motives of God, and he presented a counterargument that eating the forbidden fruit would actually be a good thing. This wisdom made sense to Eve, and she bought into it to her ruin. That's the way demonic wisdom works. It seems right to us, but it leads to death and destruction when we act on it.

James exposes the operating system of such wisdom when he describes it as "earthly" and "sensual" (James 3:15). "Earthly" suggests originating with man without respect to God. "Sensual" refers to what is limited to the natural world and unspiritual. The origin of demonic counsel is this fallen world—of the flesh, not of the Spirit. It may have an appearance of godliness but is empty of power. This so-called wisdom (I imagine James would have used air quotes if he were reading out loud) is corrosive to a godly life, counterfeit to the truth, and counterproductive to Christlikeness.

This alleged wisdom is showcased by its divisive, disorderly, destructive effects: "But if you have bitter envy and self-seeking in your hearts, do not boast and lie against the truth. This wisdom does not descend from above, but is earthly, sensual, demonic. For where envy and self-seeking exist, confusion and every evil thing are there" (James 3:14–16). Rather than bringing blessing, health, and peace, demonic wisdom plays to self-interest and self-sufficiency and ends up being contrary to the kingdom ends we are to seek.

When we hear of demonic wisdom and see its aftermath, we may breathe a sigh of relief and thank God that has nothing to do with us. The thing is, if we are honest with ourselves, we often see bitter jealousy and selfish ambition at work in us. Rather than humility, we boast in ourselves. We engage in practices that are vile to our calling in Christ, more in keeping with Satan than our Savior. In our relationships, we become troublemakers rather than peacemakers. In our self-service, we use others. In our self-sufficiency, we take our eyes off Christ and try to go it alone. In our stubborn rebellion, we can harden our hearts and suffer the consequences of which our Lord has so graciously warned us.

Where have we bought into the lies of our enemy the devil? Where have we given over the members of our body, including our tongue (James 3:6), as instruments of unrighteousness? Where do we see evidence of pride in ourselves that resists the will of God and invites the foothold of Satan into our lives? It is in the mirror of God's Word and by the conviction of the Holy Spirit that we are able to discern these things and turn to Christ as our refuge and strength.

DOING THE WORD

1. What are the telltale signs of demonic wisdom?
2. What can we expect when we follow such wisdom?

Chapter 35

A Yield of Good Fruits

The fruit of righteousness is sown in peace.
—JAMES 3:18

A computer virus can be an insidious thing. Introduced into our computer via an attachment we were foolish to open or even one embedded in a harmless graphic we downloaded, its effect can be pervasive and crippling. We can no longer trust our programs to do what they should. Instead of enjoying the organization our computers give us, we experience disorder and frustration. We lose productivity until the virus is expelled and working order is restored.

That dysfunction is what we experience in life when we introduce what James calls wisdom that is "earthly, sensual, demonic" (James 3:15). Buying in to what seems right to us or what secular culture is offering can lead to all sorts of difficulties, but particularly such foolishness disguised as wisdom does not honor God or yield the blessing He intends (see the contrast of wisdom versus foolishness of Psalm 1).

Contrasted with demonic wisdom is wisdom that descends from above (James 3:15). Clearly, James has in mind wisdom that comes from God. This wisdom is tied in to the written Word that God has provided for us and the discernment and discretion that come from the Holy Spirit, a wisdom that is ours for the asking (1:5). Such wisdom comes from God, walks with God, and seeks the glory of God. It transforms us and our circumstances, whether in the difficulties of trials or the routine conduct of our lives.

Demonic wisdom leads to disorder and dysfunction. Wisdom from above produces a quite different result: "But the wisdom that is from above is first pure, then peaceable, gentle, willing to yield, full of mercy and good fruits, without partiality and without hypocrisy. Now the fruit of righteousness is sown in peace by those who make peace" (James 3:17–18).

James begins by describing this wisdom as pure, even giving purity a position of first importance. We might think of "purity" in terms of chastity, where we are fully and exclusively devoted to God. Everything about us is sacred, set apart as holy to our God. That's how wisdom operates from the perspective of the fear of the Lord. From the starting point of purity, the operating system of wisdom works itself out in all the fruit of saving faith forged by the Spirit of God and founded in the person of Christ. Gentleness serves well as a trait of the tongue. Notice how Paul uses "gentle" as a governor to our speech: "to speak evil of no one, to be peaceable, gentle, showing all humility to all men" (Titus 3:2).

Wisdom that comes from God will lead us in being "willing to yield" (James 3:17). Rather than being pigheaded in prideful arrogance, we will display a readiness to listen, a slowness to speak, and a willingness to be persuaded. In other words, in our relationships we will readily exercise the royal law of loving others as we love ourselves.

James presents the image of a rich crop cultivated by the grace of God, abounding in mercy, resplendent with good fruit, diverse with an impartiality that leaves room for the diversity of God's image bearers, and producing fruit that is authentic, abounding, and abiding. Such is the kingdom crop sown by wisdom from above that loves God and neighbor. James labels this crop a "harvest of righteousness" (James 3:18 ESV).

It all begins with setting our eyes on God and seeking His glory (see the prayer of Phil. 1:9–11). We want to sow in our minds and in our relationships what we want to harvest in our lives. The seed we reach to scatter must be taken from the bag marked "Wisdom from Above," not "Wisdom That Is Demonic." Both stand open before us.

DOING THE WORD

1. What are the hallmarks of wisdom from above?
2. What will produce a harvest of righteousness?

Chapter 36

At the Core of Conflict

Where do wars and fights come from?
—JAMES 4:1

Check out just about any social media thread, and you'll see that even the most innocuous of posts can devolve into uncivil discourse and personal attack. People don't hesitate to tear others down rather than engage in a respectful exchange of ideas. Extreme disregard of others along with preoccupation with self and assertion of rights can easily result in road rage, flight rage, and outrage. Most disturbing is when those who claim to follow Jesus Christ act in kind. Their behavior is often indistinguishable from those who belong to the kingdom of darkness.

We can detect a theme in James. He has urged us to kingdom decorum—loving others, respecting them, and serving them in the manner of our Lord Jesus. We have just seen that he has been aghast at the notion we would use our tongues to curse others, those made in the image of God. The idea that we would look down on others has been repugnant to him.

James turns to examine the cause of quarrels. By way of answer, he points the finger of blame directly at us: "Where do wars and fights come from among you? Do they not come from your desires for pleasure that war in your members? You lust and do not have. You murder and covet and cannot obtain. You fight and war. Yet you do not have because you do not ask" (James 4:1–2). When we talk about the behavior of others on social media, James would have us take a look in the mirror and ask ourselves if we are corralling the same impulses in ourselves that we see in others.

What James says hearkens back to what our Lord taught in the Sermon on the Mount. There He urged us to seek first the kingdom of God and His righteousness. James, however, notes that because we often give leeway to covetousness and evil desires, we end up seeking our own glory and righteousness. This worldly ambition often pits us against others, where we try to lord it over them rather than love and serve them in the model of our Lord Jesus Christ.

Our self-centeredness even pits us against God. James exposes the root problem: "You ask and do not receive, because you ask amiss, that you may spend it on your pleasures. Adulterers and adulteresses! Do you not know that friendship with the world is enmity with God? Whoever therefore wants to be a friend of the world makes himself an enemy of God" (James 4:3–4). What a shocking and upsetting thought—pitting ourselves against God! Yet that is just what we do when we are driven by our glory, our pleasure, and our own will. James is reiterating a principle he introduced early on when he spoke of a double-minded man not receiving anything from the Lord (1:7–8). God wants our hearts, the whole of our hearts.

When James uses the terms "adulterers" and "adulteresses" (James 4:4), he is not slinging insults as happens on social media. Rather, he is bringing a wisdom perspective to bear. Adultery speaks to being unfaithful to the God to whom we pledged our troth. We commit spiritual adultery whenever we give our heart to another. This sacred relationship and our vows to follow Christ are the backdrop to James's question: "Or do you think that the Scripture says in vain, 'The Spirit who dwells in us yearns jealously'"? (v. 5).

Our relationship with God reaches to all of life, from exchanges on social media, to the work we do, to our use of time. The royal law of loving our neighbor as ourselves grows from the soil of the greatest commandment of loving the Lord our God with all our heart, soul, and mind.

DOING THE WORD

1. Whose interests are served by your quarrels and conflicts?
2. What does it mean for God to be jealous for your allegiance?

Chapter 37

Power in Weakness

Resist the devil.

—JAMES 4:7

It's natural to expect that the larger army or the force with greater weaponry would defeat a smaller or less well-equipped one. Jesus suggested as much in His teaching on discipleship (Luke 14:26–33). But that is not how it works with spiritual warfare.

As we've seen, every trial carries with it a struggle against an unseen enemy who wages war for our hearts. In the trials God brings to refine us in the image of His Son, a spiritual adversary is at work to distance us from God and even pit us against Him. This enemy wants to thwart God's purpose for us by urging unbelief that neither sees God nor seeks Him in our adversity.

James and every other New Testament writer operate with the perspective that Satan and his demons oppose us because we bear the name of Christ. Our Lord Jesus reminds us that this antagonism is expected while we sojourn between here and glory. In His High Priestly Prayer that concludes His time with His disciples in the upper room before heading out to Gethsemane, Jesus prayed this to the Father: "I do not pray that You should take them out of the world, but that You should keep them from the evil one" (John 17:15).

James equips us to deal with this spiritual adversary. After contrasting the world being at enmity with God and calling us to allegiance to God, James ministers to us in our struggle:

> But He gives more grace. Therefore He says:
> "God resists the proud,
> But gives grace to the humble."
>
> Therefore submit to God. Resist the devil and he will

> flee from you. Draw near to God and He will draw near to you. Cleanse your hands, you sinners; and purify your hearts, you double-minded. Lament and mourn and weep! Let your laughter be turned to mourning and your joy to gloom. Humble yourselves in the sight of the Lord, and He will lift you up. (James 4:6–10)

In these verses, James lays out tenets for waging spiritual warfare. He begins by having us look to the God who is for us, who "gives more grace" (James 4:6; Greek, *mega*). God is our sufficiency in the fray, and He is lavish in dispensing all that we need to stand up to the devil. It is not through a great army or cutting-edge weaponry or ingenious strategy that we will prevail (see Ps. 33:16–22). Our power is not found in might but in meekness, much as Paul learned in the struggles he faced: "My grace is sufficient for you, for My strength is made perfect in weakness" (2 Cor. 12:9). It is in weakness that Paul and we find that our strength is in the Lord our God.

We wage spiritual battle not with the bravado of pride but with complete dependence on our God (James 4:6). In the battle plan James outlines, he shows us what it looks like to humble ourselves (vv. 7–8). We *submit* ourselves to God, deferring to His rule and provision. We *resist* the devil, standing against his temptations, deceptions, accusations, and ambitions. We *draw near* to God, with the promise that He will be with us and for us as our fortress, shield, and strength (Ps. 18:1–3). We *cleanse* our hands and *purify* our hearts from double-mindedness, repentant of our waywardness, and confident in the victory of Christ, through which Satan is disarmed, defeated, and repelled.

DOING THE WORD

1. How does double-mindedness play into the devil's hands?
2. How do we find power in weakness against our spiritual foe?

Chapter 38

Judge Not

There is one Lawgiver.

—JAMES 4:12

In chapter 3 James gave us an analysis of the tongue, showing us its destructive potential. He moved on to expose the instability of our hearts beset with bitter envy and selfish ambition, where he urged us to seek wisdom from God that is peaceable, gentle, and willing to yield. Such wisdom will handle the tongue safely. In chapter 4, James again touches on what causes quarrels and conflict with others. Now, he gives the practical counsel of not using our tongue to tear down others and incite conflict: "Do not speak evil of one another, brethren" (v. 11). He says this on the heels of calling us to humility. We are not to exalt ourselves above others.

Speaking evil can refer to slander, accusation, or general toxic speech that tears others down. James uses the expression three times in this single verse. He goes on to tell us why speaking evil is out of place for us: "He who speaks evil of a brother and judges his brother, speaks evil of the law and judges the law. But if you judge the law, you are not a doer of the law but a judge" (James 4:11). When we judge others, we elevate ourselves above the law, when we ourselves are under the same Lord as those we judge. Our Lord Jesus addressed this in the Sermon on the Mount when He said, "Judge not, that you be not judged" (Matt. 7:1).

How many times have we heard people excuse and enable wrong behavior by saying that the Bible tells us not to judge? But the Bible doesn't say that. In fact, we are enjoined to judge: "For what have I to do with judging those also who are outside? Do you not judge those who are inside? But those who are outside God judges. Therefore 'put away from yourselves the evil person'" (1 Cor. 5:12–13). Judging is part of church discipline (Matt. 18:15–20). We judge when we discriminate between right and wrong, truth and error.

What the Bible does say is that we are not to judge with differing weights. We are not to hold one standard for ourselves and another standard for someone else. That's called hypocrisy. People quote "Judge not, that you be not judged," but neglect the rest of the story: "For with what judgment you judge, you will be judged; and with the measure you use, it will be measured back to you. And why do you look at the speck in your brother's eye, but do not consider the plank in your own eye?" (Matt. 7:2–3).

In other words, we are not to judge as the Judge. We both, the judged and the judging, find ourselves under the same Lord. As James put it, "There is one Lawgiver, who is able to save and to destroy. Who are you to judge another?" (James 4:12). Any judging we do is always to be done in humility, knowing that we too are sinners, and it is only by the grace of God that we go, as James has made clear (v. 6).

Often, we speak evil against others because we think we occupy the moral high ground. Peter presses the same point about not lording it over others:

> Likewise you younger people, submit yourselves to your elders. Yes, all of you be submissive to one another, and be clothed with humility, for
> "God resists the proud,
> But gives grace to the humble." (1 Peter 5:5)

The call to humility is for both those in authority and those under authority because we all have one Lord.

DOING THE WORD

1. How would you respond to someone who insists that Jesus said not to judge?
2. Why are we so prone to judge others?

Chapter 39

Planning in Pencil

You do not know what will happen tomorrow.

—JAMES 4:14

My wife and I had a well-planned, web-researched, reservation-booked, mostly paid-for trip to Ireland all set up for 2020. Then COVID hit with a vengeance. Countries shut down. Plans were scuttled. The good news is that we were able to recoup all the money we laid out. Also good news is that our shelved itinerary sits at the ready for when I muster the ambition to try again.

All of us can relate to this scenario, whether for plans big or small. James's counsel to us is this:

> Come now, you who say, "Today or tomorrow we will go to such and such a city, spend a year there, buy and sell, and make a profit"; whereas you do not know what will happen tomorrow. For what is your life? It is even a vapor that appears for a little time and then vanishes away. Instead you ought to say, "If the Lord wills, we shall live and do this or that." (James 4:13–15)

James is not saying that we should not plan. Rather, he is urging us to plan in pencil, ready to erase or revise. The point is not merely adjusting to unforeseen circumstances like COVID, but submitting ourselves and our plans to God. Involved is more than what we include on our calendars. It is the perspective we bring to life as believers. James opened his letter by telling us to consider it all joy when we encounter trials of various kinds. None of us have trials noted in our monthly planners, but we know that we will encounter trials of various kinds that will be entered in our calendars by the hand of our God.

We should want to open our hearts and submit our wills to whatever life may hold under the providence of God. That is the perspective of wisdom. Wisdom may not understand the why but does recognize all that comes to pass serves the will of our Father in heaven and carries His perfect purpose for us in it.

Wisdom is not static; it is dynamic. As the saying goes, you can't steer a parked car. Wisdom is the firm hand on the steering wheel that acts and reacts with respect to God. Oriented around the fear of the Lord, wisdom negotiates the twists and turns of life in recognition of the sovereign Lord, in deference to His secret will, and in compliance with His revealed will.

Moses juxtaposed these two aspects when he wrote, "The secret things belong to the LORD our God, but those things which are revealed belong to us and to our children forever, that we may do all the words of this law" (Deut. 29:29). The secret things are hidden to us, not to God, but they are there, at work. The revealed things have been written down for us to take into account and obey. Both aspects are embraced by faith.

The problem is when we buck against our creaturely limitations and become discontent with not knowing or malcontent when our plans are waylaid. We would do well to remember and embrace that we are a vapor that vanishes and entrust ourselves and the course of our lives to God. Our Lord Jesus incorporates this perspective as part of our daily prayer:

> Our Father in heaven,
> Hallowed be Your name.
> Your kingdom come.
> Your will be done
> On earth as it is in heaven.
> (Matt. 6:9–10)

DOING THE WORD

1. What does it mean to plan in pencil?
2. How can you yield your calendar to God?

God Willing

If the Lord wills ...
—JAMES 4:15

I have noted that the overriding pastoral concern of James's letter has to do with faith. Faith is not freestanding. It is always *in* something. The Christian's faith is in God. James's concern echoes the foundational feature of faith spoken of by the writer of Hebrews: "Without faith it is impossible to please Him, for he who comes to God must believe that He is, and that He is a rewarder of those who diligently seek Him" (Heb. 11:6). By faith we realize that we are but dust, a vapor that appears for a time and then vanishes (James 4:14). By faith we recognize that God is the creator and we are the created. By faith we entrust ourselves to our faithful God, knowing that He does all things well. Such realizations are the antidote to arrogance. Prideful unbelief is the essence of sin.

This Creator-creature distinction undergirds James's teaching about planning. James doesn't discourage our planning, just our writing those plans in pen as though they were indelible. Rather, we are to subject our plans to the will of our Father in heaven. As James put it, "Instead you ought to say, 'If the Lord wills, we shall live and do this or that.' But now you boast in your arrogance. All such boasting is evil" (James 4:15–16).

What is it James wants us to understand? Is it simply that things change, and we need to be ready to adjust? Certainly that's true, but there is a more fundamental matter to consider: there is only one God, and it's not us. In Psalm 90, the only psalm attributed to Moses, the concluding plea is,

> And let the beauty of the LORD our God be upon us,
> And establish the work of our hands for us;
> Yes, establish the work of our hands. (v. 17)

Whatever our to-do list holds, whatever plan we make to "go to such and such a city, spend a year there, buy and sell, and make a profit" (James 4:13), the success and lasting value of our efforts depend on the blessing of our God.

Moses arrives at his plea for God to establish the work of his hands on the basis of the Creator-creature distinction. Early in the psalm he says,

> Before the mountains were brought forth,
> Or ever You had formed the earth and the world,
> Even from everlasting to everlasting, You are God.
> (90:2)

Moses does not just describe God as everlasting; He is "from everlasting to everlasting." That is a poetic way of saying that God is without beginning and without end. Even the concept of unfolding time ("from... to...") is swallowed up in the immutable, self-existent being of God.

In contrast we are finite beings, enclosed in time, whose being is not inherent but derived (Acts 17:28). Moses gives us a taste of our condition when he says of God, "You return man to dust and say, 'Return, O children of man!'" (Psalm 90:3 ESV).

It is this Creator-creature distinction that James wants us to understand and to operate in light of. "You do not know what will happen tomorrow. For what is your life? It is even a vapor that appears for a little time and then vanishes away" (James 4:14; see also Ps. 90:5–6). The octane for a faith-fueled life finds its potency in humble submission to and reliance on our Creator God.

DOING THE WORD

1. What is the Creator-creature distinction?
2. How does this distinction help us to walk by faith?

Money Matters

Come now, you rich.
—JAMES 5:1

My guess is that we won't find James 5:1 in one of those verse-a-day packets: "Come now, you rich, weep and howl for your miseries that are coming upon you!" (James 5:1). Yet that verse, with the contrast it presents, captures the tension we face each day as disciples of Jesus Christ, seeking of first importance the kingdom of God and His righteousness.

Earlier in his letter, James discouraged believers from discrimination on the basis of station. He said we should not give preference in the assembly to a man wearing fine clothes over someone sporting shabby clothing. He warned us against the sin of partiality and called us to love and respect others. In his instruction to the believers, James took a swipe at the rich: "Do not the rich oppress you and drag you into the courts?" (James 2:6).

Now, as he winds down his letter, James addresses the rich themselves: "Come now, you rich, weep and howl for your miseries that are coming upon you! Your riches are corrupted, and your garments are moth-eaten. Your gold and silver are corroded, and their corrosion will be a witness against you and will eat your flesh like fire. You have heaped up treasure in the last days" (James 5:1–3). James pulls no punches in castigating the rich.

What is James's problem with those who have wealth? The problem is not their money but their love of money and how that works itself out in their treatment of others:

> Indeed the wages of the laborers who mowed your fields, which you kept back by fraud, cry out; and the cries of the reapers have reached the ears of the Lord of Sabaoth. You

> have lived on the earth in pleasure and luxury; you have fattened your hearts as in a day of slaughter. You have condemned, you have murdered the just; he does not resist you. (James 5:4–6)

James describes these rich men as loving things and using people rather than loving people and using things. They operate in a manner contrary to the kingdom of God. They disregard a basic tenet of what it means to follow Jesus Christ: "No one can serve two masters; for either he will hate the one and love the other, or else he will be loyal to the one and despise the other. You cannot serve God and mammon" (Matt. 6:24). "Mammon" refers to money or possessions and represents a kingdom and a king contrary to the kingdom of God.

James's problem with the rich is not their money but their master. In serving money they oppressed the poor, ran roughshod over the helpless, and exploited whomever they could for their own gain. Rejecting the model of the Master, they sought to be served rather than to serve.

How are those who have wealth to live? They are to live under the lordship of Christ, store up treasure in heaven, and use their means to help meet the needs of others (2 Cor. 8:8–9; 9:7–13) as an exercise of lively faith. James would echo the amen to the admonition from the pen of the apostle Paul:

> Command those who are rich in this present age not to be haughty, nor to trust in uncertain riches but in the living God, who gives us richly all things to enjoy. Let them do good, that they be rich in good works, ready to give, willing to share, storing up for themselves a good foundation for the time to come, that they may lay hold on eternal life. (1 Tim. 6:17–19)

DOING THE WORD

1. Why does God care about how we use our money?
2. How does your handling of money reflect your heart's ambition?

Patient in Affliction

Establish your hearts.

—JAMES 5:8

Now James begins to draw his letter to a close: "Therefore be patient, brethren, until the coming of the Lord" (James 5:7). James has moved from addressing the rich in verses 1–6 to speaking to all the brothers, just as he did when he began his letter (1:2). The entire household of faith is in view.

In addition to the wider audience, James brings to bear wider instruction. "Therefore" is a connecting word that builds on what has been said and leads to a conclusion or consequence. James could be building on what he has just said to the rich, but his address to all the brothers suggests that the "therefore" relates not merely to the immediate context but to the entirety of his letter, all that he has written about trials and wisdom and being doers of the word.

What application does James bring to us in the "therefore" that could bear the weight of his entire letter? He calls us to patience in affliction. Patience involves more than resigning ourselves to suffering, looking to bide our time and tough it out. Rather, as James told the brethren from the start, we are to rejoice in our trials because of what we know by faith.

Patience suggests waiting. How long are we to be patient? James tells us "until the coming of the Lord." There will come a day when wrongs will be made right, oppression will cease, and suffering will be no more. It's all tied in to the reality of the kingdom of Jesus Christ that is already present and will one day be ushered in in fullness.

In true pastoral fashion, James drives home his admonition with an illustration: "See how the farmer waits for the precious fruit of the earth, waiting patiently for it until it receives the early and latter rain" (James

5:7). The sense is that we cannot rush the Lord's hand, but we can be certain that He will bring about relief and renewal in His time (see similar theme and imagery in Joel 2:26–27). Such waiting is pregnant with expectation and promise. We don't merely wait; we wait on the Lord. James reminds us that our suffering is but for a while. A greater day is in store for those who love God (James 5:8; 1 Peter 5:10–11).

The patience James calls for and illustrates in verse 7 he repeats in verse 8, again directing our eyes to the coming of the Lord: "You also be patient. Establish your hearts, for the coming of the Lord is at hand." In addition to the endurance and longsuffering of patience in affliction, James adds another element: "Establish your hearts." The sense is "to make firm." In the face of adversity, we must burrow ourselves more deeply into the everlasting arms of our Lord. We double down on the hope that is ours in Christ. We are reminded that faith has a foundation, a firm foundation. Those who hope in Christ will not be disappointed.

DOING THE WORD

1. What is your greatest struggle in dealing with suffering?
2. How do we exercise patience as we wait on the Lord?

Chapter 43

Persevering Faith

Count them blessed who endure.

—JAMES 5:11

When we are in the midst of suffering, it's hard to get our bearings. Sometimes it seems it's all we can do to put one foot in front of the other. We can become disoriented in the fog of not knowing what's going on and a bit frantic as we try to manage all that is coming at us. James, however, gives us the bearings we need to move on and make the most of what he has characterized as an opportunity for our spiritual growth. Just as He reassured the Israelites in their wilderness wandering of His presence with the shekinah glory (Ex. 13:21–22), God wants us to know that He is with us. He wants us to see His glory and trust His good providence as we navigate uncharted and often inhospitable terrain.

Being steadfast in suffering makes certain requirements of us. In our affliction James urges us, "Do not grumble against one another, brethren, lest you be condemned. Behold, the Judge is standing at the door!" (James 5:9). Perhaps James had in mind those times when the Israelites complained against God in the desert and suffered the consequences for their rebellion. The important thing is that we rest in our God in the midst of adversity, not grumbling or complaining, not faultfinding, but seeking a contentment in His will in any and every circumstance. That's the way faith works. We have a whole wing of the Bible dedicated to its display in Hebrews 11, where we see saints of old pressing on in hardship because they knew and believed God.

To help us on our way, James holds up for us two Old Testament examples: "My brethren, take the prophets, who spoke in the name of the Lord, as an example of suffering and patience. Indeed we count them blessed who endure" (James 5:10–11). Many of the prophets of old suffered greatly in the conduct of their duties but by faith pressed on in service to God and confidence in His promises. The writer of Hebrews describes what some of these endured:

> Others were tortured, not accepting deliverance, that they might obtain a better resurrection. Still others had trial of mockings and scourgings, yes, and of chains and imprisonment. They were stoned, they were sawn in two, were tempted, were slain with the sword. They wandered about in sheepskins and goatskins, being destitute, afflicted, tormented. (11:35–37)

These examples should disabuse us of thinking that as Christians we are exempt from suffering (see Matt. 5:11–12).

In James's second example from the Old Testament, we find the epitome of suffering: "You have heard of the perseverance of Job and seen the end intended by the Lord—that the Lord is very compassionate and merciful" (James 5:11). In the blink of an eye, all that Job held dear—his children, his possessions, his health—were taken away. How did Job respond? He struggled as we would, wrestling with confusion, grief, anger, and the like. But overriding Job's struggle were two pillars: trust in the Lord for today (Job 1:21) and bright hope for tomorrow (19:25–26).

James holds up for us the prophets of old and Job not only to give us examples by seeing how they persevered in suffering but also to give us encouragement by seeing the God who preserves. In these examples we see the purpose of God at work, and we are reminded of His character, that He is full of compassion and mercy despite appearances to the contrary.

DOING THE WORD

1. What does it mean to be steadfast in suffering?
2. How does faith help navigate the storms of adversity?

Chapter 44

Swear Not

Above all, my brethren, do not swear.

—JAMES 5:12

James continues to wrap up his letter. He addresses all the believers and calls us to patience and perseverance in trial. But now he writes something that seems very much a non sequitur: "But above all, my brethren, do not swear, either by heaven or by earth or with any other oath. But let your 'Yes' be 'Yes,' and your 'No,' 'No,' lest you fall into judgment" (James 5:12).

We struggle to see how this verse fits into James's flow of thought. It seems rather random. He has been talking about suffering (5:10) and goes on talking about it (v. 13), but in verse 12 it's as though he is interrupting himself. To make matters more confusing, not only does James introduce a seemingly extraneous topic, but also he elevates it to a place of supreme importance. He says, "Above all." It's like a piece from another jigsaw puzzle has gotten put in the wrong box.

If we squint, we can make verse 12 fit. After all, it does have to do with the tongue, a topic James addressed earlier. And James did just talk about grumbling (James 5:9), which relates to the tongue. In addition, James is considered the Proverbs of the New Testament, and Wisdom Literature warns against rash vows (e.g., Eccl. 5:4–5). His letter also makes many references to Christ's Sermon on the Mount, and in that sermon our Lord does talk about taking oaths (Matt. 5:34–37). So, maybe verse 12 does belong in the same box, but it's hard to see where it fits in without forcing it.

There is another possibility. Throughout his letter, James has alluded to our Lord's teaching in the Sermon on the Mount. Now, however, he virtually quotes Jesus from that sermon. In Matthew 5:34, our Lord says,

"Do not swear." He mentions heaven and earth. He says, "But let your 'Yes' be 'Yes,' and your 'No,' 'No.' For whatever is more than these is from the evil one" (v. 37). If James were giving a political speech and he made the statement he does about oaths using the same terms and phrases as Jesus does, he would be accused of plagiarism.

Perhaps what's happening is this. As James wraps up his letter, in verse 7 he broadens his address from the rich to all the brothers (like in 1:2) and uses the word "therefore" to bring to bear the content of the entire letter. Now, in verse 12, James wants us to hear the voice of Jesus in whose name he has written the letter, as he made clear at the start (1:1). Just like if we were to hear "four score and seven years ago" our thoughts would flash to Abraham Lincoln, by virtually quoting Jesus from the Sermon on the Mount, James wants us to hear Jesus. Overarching and underpinning everything he has written in his letter is the authority and pastoral concern of the Lord Jesus Christ. That's why James can say, "Above all, my brethren."

James may well be addressing the subject of oaths because he is stressing that they are unnecessary and even inappropriate because the sincerity of our word should be sufficient. But he may also be speaking against the pharisaical excesses that Jesus was taking to task in the Sermon on the Mount. If that is the case, James is telling us that not only do we need to be true to our word, but we need to be true to the word he has written in his epistle in the name of Jesus.

DOING THE WORD

1. How does serving Christ govern what you say, how you say it, and why you say it?
2. Why should we not be rash with our words?

The Prayer of Faith

Is anyone among you suffering? Let him pray.
—JAMES 5:13

James began his epistle equipping us with how to handle trials with faith: "My brethren, count it all joy when you fall into various trials, knowing that the testing of your faith produces patience" (James 1:2–3). Trials *prove* our faith by testing its mettle, showing it to be the product of the grace of God and not something that has its origin in us. Trials also *improve* our faith in the sense that the fruit of sanctification is cultivated through the handiwork of God's grace. Trials are the workstations by which the muscle of faith is strengthened, as God grows us to maturity, forming Christ in us.

Throughout his epistle James highlights genuine, saving faith compared with its presumptive counterfeit. Faith that works is faith that is effective because it belongs to the gift of salvation from God. Such faith leads us to, as Paul put it, "work out your own salvation with fear and trembling; for it is God who works in you both to will and to do for His good pleasure" (Phil. 2:12–13). Faith without works is dead, James tells us, because such faith does not exhibit the power of new life in Christ.

As he winds up his letter, James closes in prayer. It is not that he prays but that he teaches us about prayer. In James 5:13–18, James mentions prayer in every verse. He wants us to understand prayer as the voice of faith and to see the place given it by our God and Father:

> Is anyone among you suffering? Let him pray. Is anyone cheerful? Let him sing psalms. Is anyone among you sick? Let him call for the elders of the church, and let them pray over him, anointing him with oil in the name of the Lord. And the prayer of faith will save the sick, and the Lord

> will raise him up. And if he has committed sins, he will be forgiven (5:13–15).

James begins by calling us to prayer in whatever circumstance we find ourselves. Are we in distress? We are to pray, casting our cares on our God, who is full of compassion and mercy (James 5:11). Are we at ease? Let us tune our hearts to sing God's praise. Whatever our situation, we are to commune with our heavenly Father in a holy murmur of prayer.

Isn't that what we would expect of faith? Faith is not something we pull from our emergency kit in times of distress. Rather, we live by faith, a faith that knows, trusts, depends on, and seeks our Father in heaven.

What might we pray? Our heart can be our guide, lifting to God our fears, worries, and desires, being open and real before Him. But throughout his epistle, James has given us other things to pray for: joy in the midst of trial, wisdom to navigate life to God's glory, submission to His purposes, obedience to His will, protection from our enemy the devil, guarding our tongues.

Faith cannot remain silent. All we need to do is look at the saints of old and listen to their conversations with God around whatever they were experiencing. The psalms are filled with expressions of praise, confession, lament, petition, and struggles of faith. Those psalms were penned in the trenches of life lived by men who share the same struggles we do. If we need templates for our prayer, we could do no better.

DOING THE WORD

1. In what way is prayer the voice of faith?
2. Why should we pray in both good times and hard times?

Chapter 46

Power in Prayer

The effective, fervent prayer of a righteous man avails much.
—JAMES 5:16

James has urged us to seek God in whatever circumstance we find ourselves. Prayer is the voice of faith raised in praise, petition, lament, thanksgiving, and any other response to life's vicissitudes and vagaries.

But we are to pray not only for ourselves; we are to pray for others. God has given us the avenue of prayer for intercession as well as petition. This ministry of prayer belongs to those who are tasked with praying, "the elders of the church" (James 5:14), and to the church family as a whole, "one another" (v. 16).

"Is anyone among you sick? Let him call for the elders of the church, and let them pray over him, anointing him with oil in the name of the Lord" (James 5:14). James's focus here is on those who have a calling of prayer in the community of God, the elders of the church. Elders are those who are mature in the Lord, raised up by God to shepherd the flock of which He has made them overseers. They carry out their shepherding role primarily through prayer and ministry of the word (Acts 6:4) and personal example (Acts 20:28; 1 Peter 5:2–3). In a sense, the elders are professional "pray-ers," not in the sense of being paid but in that it is their ministerial call. Through prayer and the spiritual symbol of oil (James 5:14), elders lift the eyes of one beset by sin and sickness to the Healer.

James continues:

> And the prayer of faith will save the sick, and the Lord will raise him up. And if he has committed sins, he will be forgiven. Confess your trespasses to one another, and pray for one another, that you may be healed. The effective, fervent prayer of a righteous man avails much. (James 5:15–16)

The prayer of faith is not some specific prayer or special species of prayer. It is simply believing prayer, what James spoke of in chapter 1 of praying "in faith" (v. 6). Such prayer knows God, trusts God, seeks God, and expects God to hear and answer. It means that when we pray, we don't just rattle off words; we make eye contact with our God and Father, casting our cares on Him, assured that He cares for us.

James gives us great confidence that our prayers will be effective. Where does prayer gain its effectiveness? James has made it clear that all things unfold according to the will of God. Our prayer does not find its power in the prayer itself (right words, repetition), or in the one praying (pastor, elder). Rather, prayer finds its power in the decree of God, His eternal purpose that enfolds our prayers as His means for His ends. James wants us to know that our stuttering faith-fueled pleas are effective for the accomplishment of God's purposes, according to His design.

To encourage us in prayer, James holds up the Old Testament prophet Elijah: "Elijah was a man with a nature like ours, and he prayed earnestly that it would not rain; and it did not rain on the land for three years and six months. And he prayed again, and the heaven gave rain, and the earth produced its fruit" (James 5:17–18). God could have held back or brought forth the rain unilaterally, but He did so *in response to prayer*. James showcases prayer as the means by which God acted. Moreover, this avenue to the Almighty is not open only to luminaries like Elijah. James emphasizes that Elijah was a human being just like us, a man with fears and doubts, a righteous man (that is, a believer) who prayed with the fervency of faith.

DOING THE WORD

1. What is the prayer of faith?
2. How does James encourage our prayer?

Chapter 47

Truth Matters

... if anyone among you wanders from the truth ...

—JAMES 5:19

We've seen James to be an eminently practical book. The question is, do we take seriously what James has taught us? Do we buy into the idea that faith can be authentic or counterfeit? Do we believe that we can deceive ourselves with mere presumption of saving faith, being professors but not possessors? Do we believe that faith in the Lord Jesus Christ works itself out in allegiance to Him and alignment with His will, as it resists the schemes and snares of the evil one? Do we acknowledge that the gospel of the kingdom is truth and that apart from that truth there is neither life nor hope?

If we do embrace what James has taught us, then we will not be surprised by James's closing words: "Brethren, if anyone among you wanders from the truth, and someone turns him back, let him know that he who turns a sinner from the error of his way will save a soul from death and cover a multitude of sins" (James 5:19–20). In a sense, James is authenticating all that he has said before. Apart from Christ, there is no salvation. Apart from faith in Christ, a person is not saved. A profession of faith apart from works that validate that profession is nothing but presumption. Truth matters. To wander from the truth is to stray from the word of God and the Christ it reveals.

In describing someone wandering from the truth, James brings to the fore the full force of his letter. To forsake truth is to reject Jesus Christ as the way, the truth, and the life. Without Christ there is no hope of salvation. It is with this realization in mind that we feel the urgency to pursue those who have turned from the truth in order to bring them back. In so doing we will rescue them from eternal death and the penalty of their sins that they will surely face apart from Christ.

James makes it clear that pursuit of the wanderer is not only the job of the elders in their obligation to the flock. It is the responsibility of the entire family of God. James issues his charge to the "brethren" (James 5:19). We all have the role of speaking the truth in love, rebuking one another, confessing our sins to one another, and exhorting one another.

How might we pursue those straying from the truth? We can use the ordinary means of contact: calls, notes, visits. We can reach out to them in pleading love. We can listen with compassion and kindness. We can bring the Scripture to bear with gentleness and respect, with patience and instruction. While we cannot force those who have strayed from the truth to return or make them repent, we can plant the word, which is able to save the soul (James 1:21), that by God's grace it might take root and bear fruit in repentance, faith, and new obedience.

The starting point of our pursuit, however, is prayer. James has just highlighted for us the power of prayer in seeking the God who is able to do more than all we ask or could even conceive. Elijah, a man like us, prayed, and God moved remarkably. He prayed specifically (for drought and for rain). He prayed fervently, importunately, insistently.

As we pursue the wanderer for God, we must pursue God for the wanderer. Only He can grant power to the implanted word. Only He can give ears to hear that they may come to Christ and not see death but have life everlasting.

DOING THE WORD

1. Why does James close on a note of truth?
2. What wanderer from the truth will you pursue?